TO
CHINA WITH LOVE

By the same author

THE COMING OF THE BARBARIANS

THE DEER CRY PAVILION

A CURIOUS LIFE FOR A LADY, ISABELLA BIRD

TO CHINA WITH LOVE

TO
CHINA WITH LOVE

*The Lives and Times of Protestant
Missionaries in China 1860-1900*

PAT BARR

1973

DOUBLEDAY & COMPANY, INC., GARDEN CITY, NEW YORK

ISBN: 0-385-03864-X
Library of Congress Catalog Card Number 72-84888
Copyright © 1972 by Pat Barr
Printed in the United States of America
First Edition in the United States of America

To J.A.

CONTENTS

ILLUSTRATIONS

Between pages 34 and 35

Between pages 66 and 67

Between pages 98 and 99

FOREWORD

This is a true story about the sort of people whom I find interesting. They are fully charged with energies and aspirations, they dare to travel to every periphery, their devotion to a cause is sufficiently fierce for the ordinary humdrum to have no hold over them. The people of this kind in this story chose to become missionaries. Today, for many of us, their ideas are so artless as to seem almost quaint, their language so unfamiliar as to need the interpretation of modern psychology, their ambitions so over-blown as to seem practically incredible. Moreover, and as far as we can see from our twentieth-century perspective, they eventually failed in much that they tried to achieve. But these things do not diminish them for the fact remains that their dramatic attempts to change the course of China's history certainly shaped the course of many events and influenced many lives.

It is the latter aspect that I have wanted to explore most fully in this book through the personalities of the missionaries themselves. I have tried to be fair in my descriptions of the conditions and conflicts of their lives, of the work they did 'in the field' and its impact on the Chinese. I have not intended to write a definitive history of Protestant missionary endeavour in China, nor a study of evangelist psychology, nor a hagiography for the devout, nor a charade for the cynic. Simply, my aim has been to bring back to life the lacklustre, stiff-shirted figure of the missionary who was an intrinsic and influential part of every Western encroachment in the Far East.

Pat Barr

ACKNOWLEDGMENTS

I should like to express my gratitude to Richard Simon, my literary agent, Charles Latimer of Secker & Warburg, and Larry Ashmead of Doubleday & Co, for their constructive encouragement and patience while I was writing this book.

I should also like to thank Mr L. T. Lyall and Miss Irene C. King of the Overseas Missionary Fellowship, Miss Jean Woods and Miss Rosemary Keen of the Church Missionary Society, and Miss Irene Fletcher of the London Missionary Society, for their willing help.

PART ONE

The essence of history does not reside in recorded facts, but in the thoughts, emotions, ideas and aspirations of the human beings who have made it. Facts are only the outer shell, the crystallisation and materialisation of ideas and emotions.

A. De Reincourt, THE SOUL OF CHINA

CHAPTER ONE

Over the Dark Blue Sea

On Sunday 25th June 1865 a weedy, tense man with fair hair and blue eyes paced the beach at Brighton, alone. He was then thirty-three years old and unknown, his education and social background were quite unexceptional; nevertheless he had such a way of attracting money that he could easily have been a millionaire if he had set his mind to it, and such a capacity for taking initiative and inspiring others that he could have been a general, or the founder of a new colony or of a successful industrial empire in his native Yorkshire.

But this man, James Hudson Taylor, never once considered any of these possibilities because he was obsessed with a vision, one that had already ruled his life for ten years and was to do so until his death forty years later. In Taylor's vision the world was divided into two unequal parts: first, the ordered, lightened part which included the secure, sunny beach whereon he walked, the properly-dressed congregations in the nearby churches and similar congregations who were singing hymns and repenting of their sins that Sabbath morning in every corner of Christendom; second, the chaotic, larger part where pitiful, disorderly, wicked heaps of humankind struggled and died back into the fearsome darknesses of heathendom. Hudson Taylor hungered to save them all, but the focus of his passion was the unredeemed Chinese, dying without God at the rate of a million a month, as he kept telling everyone, and as he kept seeing them in his mind's eye – torrents and niagaras of them, flotsams of suffering sallow faces, jetsams of

3

pigtails swirling away towards eternal damnation so that the summer sea at Brighton was dark with them.

The mamas and papas taking the air along the promenade, the clergymen even, come down now from their pulpits and washing their pink hands in preparation for Sunday luncheon, did not suppose there was much they could do about the dire plight of the benighted Chinese on the other side of the world; but upon the troubled spirit of Hudson Taylor it was an ever-present, crushing weight. He most frequently pictured himself as one standing on a rock in the middle of that dark satanic flood and equipped with a shining life-line of salvation ready to pull out all who would but reach for it.

The task was obviously enormous and for the past year or so Taylor had quailed before it – a quailing that plunged him into ever greater excesses of 'missionary arithmetic'. He calculated that, if there were five hundred men on strategically-positioned rocks willing to devote thirty years each to the cause, there would still be at least a hundred million Chinese who had not even come within reach of a saving rope; he calculated that between last year's Missionary Conference at Perth, Scotland, and the one coming up in September, 'twelve million more in China will have passed forever beyond our reach'. But in spite of all the formidable odds Taylor made up his mind that day, or rather, as he put it, 'the Lord conquered my unbelief and I surrendered myself to God for this service'. He was to start then and there to save as many Chinese souls as he possibly could, because the Lord had bade him so to do. He stood still on the sands to write in the fly-leaf of the Bible he always carried with him: 'Prayed for twenty-four willing, skilful labourers at Brighton, 25th June 1865.'

Taylor was out of himself at that moment, shuddering at the nearness of his God and the sanctity of the mission entrusted to him. To a man in the grip of such religious ferment, choices become destiny and incidents of minor personal history are invested with immeasurable significance. Such significances are further hallowed by time and success until they blossom into legends among initiates and followers. Thus, those who wrote

4

years later about the work of the China Inland Mission which Hudson Taylor determined that day to establish, and who were, when he stood upon the sands, unborn or at least uncalled, refer to their leader's earlier life as being divided into the periods of 'Before' and 'After' Brighton.

Not that Brighton was the absolute beginning, for Hudson had had the burden of the heathen Chinese early loaded upon him by his father, James Taylor. Taylor senior, a devout, domineering man and a Methodist lay-preacher, taught his son to work unsparingly, aim high and distrust all his natural appetites. The awful presence of that watching Father, so much more terrifying even than James, was constantly evoked in the back parlour of the little chemist's shop in Barnsley, Yorkshire, where the Taylor family lived. Occasional pennies that other children spent on sweets went into the earthenware Mission Jar on the mantelpiece in practice 'for the no'es of the future'; every morning Hudson and his two sisters knelt beside their parents' four-poster bed, reddened fists tightly clutched in prayer on the bleached counterpane, and told God everything – the failure to get full marks in arithmetic, the indulgent sucking of a bull's-eye, the virtuous penny popped in the Jar.

As it turned out, Hudson had an iron will and a bubbling sense of joyous purpose that his father did not quench but to which, instead, he gave life-long direction. For James Taylor too had an obsession with that far Cathay about which so little was then known; in consequence, by the time he was twelve, frail curly-haired little Hudson was announcing that, when he grew up to be a man, he was going out to China as a missionary to save souls.

Exactly why the Taylors of Barnsley were so feverishly determined to convert the Wangs of Ningpo to their own deep, narrow brand of Christianity remains a mystery to the lay mind of today, as it was to a considerable proportion of Hudson's contemporaries. For the China Inland Mission was formed during a decade of increasing scepticism on religious matters, when there was a growing awareness among the intelligent laity that the discoveries of modern science and the old certainties of Christian doctrine

5

were not always reconcilable. It was a division clarified and later symbolised by Thomas Huxley's famous row with William Wilberforce over the full implications of Darwinism upon orthodox Christian belief. With regard to foreign missions, the new scepticism crystallised in the person of one Bishop Colenso, a missionary in Africa with a mind that was too analytical for his own comfort. He was eventually tried for heresy because he dared to publish his suspicions of the credibility gap between biblical lore and new scientific and historical knowledge. The suspicions were prompted by the simple questions put to him by his Zulu converts, questions like, 'Do you really believe the Flood covered the whole world?' and 'Was Jonah honestly swallowed whole by a whale?' There was the bolt-hole of miracle of course, under which head anything went; but 'a declining sense of the miraculous' had also already been diagnosed by the historian William Lecky as one of the ills of the 1860s.

But for the traditional, reverential missionary like Hudson Taylor these currents of inquiring, controversial scepticism represented the deliberate underminings of Satan himself. For Taylor's world was medieval in its explicitness: the hosts of light and dark did battle over the provision of funds for the China Inland Mission and the Lord protected His own with watchful solicitude.

Still riding on the exhilaration of his Brighton experience, Taylor opened the first 'China Inland Mission Account' with £10 of his own money and the absolute conviction that further offerings would multiply. They did because he was a man of practical sense and great persuasion; he sought money where it existed and the pocketbooks of the rich simply fell open at his confident coming. One of the homes he visited in the cause was Langley Park, the country seat of Sir Thomas and Lady Beauchamp. The visit furnished a background for a homily that is a gem among the many that cluster about Taylor's memorial halo; it survived unflawed from its first telling in 1865 to, incredibly, 1908 when it was published in his official biography.

'So warm was the sympathy [of the Beauchamps] that they desired to help the Mission financially, though no appeal had been made for money and no collection taken. All the more perhaps for this reason Mr Taylor's host and hostess wished to give as a matter of privilege; but their generosity in other directions had left them little in hand for the purpose. After praying over it however, the thought suggested itself: "Why not trust the Lord about the conservatories and contribute to the Mission the amount almost due for their insurance?" Langley Park possessed extensive greenhouses and winter storms were apt to be serious near that east coast. But definitely committing the matter to Him who controls wind and wave, the cheque was drawn and the insurance premium paid into the Mission treasury. The sequel Mr Taylor never heard till long after, nor indeed that the gift had been made possible in this way. But the Lord knew; and when a few months later a storm of exceptional violence broke over the neighbourhood, He did not forget. Much glass was shattered for miles around, but the conservatories of Langley Park entirely escaped.'

People whose minds moved in these ways were splendid missionary material, for the natives they sought to convert also had their gods of wind and wave able to dispense retributive thunderbolts upon the over-assured and gracious dispensations upon those insured by faith alone. In this sense, at least, heathen and missionary moved within the same plain – a darkling one bounded by stern absolutes but resonant with meaning. So Hudson Taylor bestrode his faith confidently; it was to him a stallion, immensely strong and resilient; he could go anywhere on it and do anything.

'A Lecture on China and the Chinese, by Rev H. Taylor MRCS' read the poster plastered on the walls of many provincial towns throughout England during the latter part of 1865. 'The Lecture will embrace the geography, antiquity and population of the Empire and the manners, customs, languages and religion of the people and will be largely ILLUSTRATED BY MAPS, DRAWINGS, IDOLS, ARTICLES OF DRESS and other objects of interest brought from China. ADMISSION FREE. NO COLLECTION.' This last was a considered policy of Taylor's; he never took a formal collection after his meetings, but 'relied on the Lord' to provide for the Mission's needs through those who felt 'the call to give'. It was a source that never completely failed him though he skirted penury several times. One of the more reliable factors in Taylor's favour was that he, like a later evangelist Billy Graham, had a natural gift for public relations. He early understood the value of visual aids, of combining the pill of missionary recruitment with sweetening stories about the exotic, wonderful but bereft Chinese. Not that he lacked sincerity, nor that he was falsifying in any way his knowledge of China. He had already spent seven years in the country as the first English agent of the Chinese Evangelisation Society, and was well acquainted with its 'customs, languages', etc., though his understanding of China was never straight but refracted through his obsession with its 'pervasive and hopeless heathenism'.

In the wake of Taylor's arduous lecture tours, funds poured in and a number of eager applicants for the new missionary venture turned up at the terrace house in London's East End where Hudson lived with his wife, Maria, and their four children. 'Men and women of moderate ability and limited attainments are not precluded from engaging in the work,' Taylor wrote in an early exhortatory pamplet, *China – Its Spiritual Needs and Claims*. It was a more lenient, open-ended approach to missionary recruitment that provided a new outlet for devout men of the working and lower-middle classes who had insufficient academic and social qualifications for some of the most respectable societies, and for women of all classes who, as usual, had trouble in being accepted anywhere.

Among the first group of missionaries Taylor selected to go with him to China were a stonemason, a draper, two blacksmiths, two governesses, two carpenters, and three single women from prosperous families. They belonged to several different religious denominations, but seemed confidently knit together by the romance, challenge and enthusiasm of Taylor's apostolic vision. They were all fellow-workers, Taylor wrote, who, 'irrespective of denominational views fully held the inspiration of God's words and were willing to prove their faith by going to inland China with only the guarantee they carried within the covers of their pocket Bibles'. No contracts, no vacations, no fixed salaries were offered, for 'we cannot afford to have unconsecrated money at all, even to buy food with, for there are plenty of ravens in China and the Lord could send them again with bread and flesh . . .'

Figurations such as these were feasts indeed to many an ardent young soul in the English provinces who had been roused by the quickening of the evangelical revivalist movement during the 1860s but had only intensity, earnestness and courage to offer it. Will Rudland, for instance, a blacksmith's assistant of Cambridge-shire who had the text 'Quench not the Spirit' emblazoned above his forge fire. He had been converted by his former Sunday school teacher and, it was later written of him, became burdened with the crying needs of the heathen. He got hold of a book on Chinese and tried to study it in the evenings by forge firelight; ravens he saw over the autumnal fields and longed to commit himself recklessly to their care. So he went to the East End to see Hudson Taylor and was accepted as a recruit – he, who had never until then been as far as London, sailed for Shanghai with the first group of China Inland Mission missionaries the following spring.

The group was made up of fifteen recruits, plus Maria and Hudson Taylor and their family – all of them pious, plucky, high-spirited, untried and young. Hudson himself, at thirty-four, was senior and absolute leader; his wife, twenty-nine years old, a missionary's daughter whom Hudson had first met in Ningpo, took on the role of mother-confessor, mainstay and peacemaker. She was a whole-hearted woman who rejoiced and rested in her absolute faith; like her husband, she was also resourceful and prudent. 'I have had my dark blue dress re-made,' she told her mother just before sailing, '. . . but the velvet trimmings at the bottom are not necessary any more.' And, to Emily Blatchley, who acted as Taylor's secretary, 'Please, dearie, get the white petticoat done and off today. I want to take it as a pattern to get more of the Indian long-cloths . . .'

Emily, receiving that, may have gone into a tizzy, for she was highly strung and over-conscientious; she was also intelligent, dumpy and destined for a short unhappy life. Her bosom friend was Jennie Faulding, a financier's daughter, who was energetic, pretty and always singing. She lived long and eventually married the man Emily secretly worshipped. At the beginning, however, the only other married couple in the group were a Mr and Mrs Lewis Nicol from Arbroath, Scotland. Nicol, the other black-smith, had written in his letter of application, 'My heart bleeds and burns within me for the perishing multitudes in China . . . It seems to me I could endure any amount of suffering or privation although it were but to save one single soul . . .' These overwrought conventional phrases apparently impressed Taylor, though Nicol's capacity for the endurance of 'privation' turned out to be limited. An obstinate, whining, social climber, Nicol soon proved a thorn in the firm flesh of Taylor's dedication.

Pricks of dissension and quiet heartbreak, joyous singing, illness and death were all implicit in the enterprise, and this the group must have understood as they 'Launched out into the Deep' (to use the words of Taylor's biography) on 26th May 1866. They sailed for China in the *Lammermuir*, a three-masted iron wind-jammer of 760 tons and a vessel long remembered, for the shining mantle of pioneering heroism was quickly bestowed upon the '*Lammermuir* Party' by the faithful watchers left at home and admiring recruits who later followed a similar route.

They felt themselves to be spiritual pilgrims of the *Mayflower* variety, for they were sternly pious, aggressive, obsessed with prayer, self-confident and self-conscious. Taylor, with his flair for publicity, ensured that photographs commemorating the depar-ture were on sale at the Mission's London headquarters within a few months – the whole party enlarged for one shilling; individual portraits, sixpence each. Jennie Faulding, writing to her parents two years after, confessed, 'I still have the dear old *Lammermuir* label on my trunk and I cannot bear to take it off, for it still makes me a little proud. I hope that is not wrong of me.' Grattan Guinness, an Irish evangelist who had been deeply impressed with Hudson Taylor's magnetic personality, later wrote a commemora-tive poem about the sailing of the *Lammermuir*. It begins:

Over the dark blue sea, over the trackless flood
A little band has gone in the service of their God.
The lonely waste of waters they traverse to proclaim

In the distant land of Sinim Immanuel's Saving Name.
They have heard from the far-off East the voice of their
brother's blood:
A million a month in China are dying without God.

The spirit of the whole endeavour is there: its romance and its
danger; the exclusive smallness and seeming vulnerability of the
'little band'; the emphasis on self-sacrifice and service; the plan-
gent use of the word 'blood'. Blood was a much-used word in
missionary literature of the nineteenth century, with its hallowed
echoing back to so many of the biblical stories that the devout
knew by heart, and its thrilling, terrible intimations of physical
violence and sacrifice even unto martyrdom. Eventually there
were to be blood-stained Christian martyrs in the land of Sinim,
and blood was fairly soon to be shed in the cause, but foreknow-
ledge of this would not for a moment have deterred the 'little
band'.

One, at least, of their number – Will Rudland, the Cambridge-
shire blacksmith – survived until 1912, the year in which the
Manchu dynasty of China was overthrown and the new Chinese
Republic began the long march into godless Communism. Knowledge of this fact might have shaken the group's trust in the
ultimate efficacy of the Divine Protection, but in 1866 no wisp of
Communism tainted the horizons and their mainstay was secure:
God, who watched over the Langley Park conservatories, would
watch over them too when the tempests came. The *Lammermuir*
launched out towards distant Shanghai and its decks and cabins
rang with confident hymns of praise.

CHAPTER TWO

The Distant Land of Sinim

China, in the year 1866, stank in its every part as it always had. It was a medieval-size stink that could be tasted as well as smelt and it was made up of putrefying corpses in stagnant canals, faeces smeared over paddy-fields, decayed garbage, overflowing sewers, sun-rotted animal viscera. Introduction by omnipresent effluvia is fitting because it was the very first assault on the senses of every arriving Westerner and, as he recoiled in nausea, his every pore told him he had come to a backward, primitive country. This was not so, but the stink of China did have several implications that it was advisable for every foreign newcomer to remember: that diseases such as typhoid, cholera, smallpox were rife; that the people were thrifty and diligent enough to use their own faeces as manure; that no Chinaman with any social commonsense would ever fish a drowning or dead man out of a canal because this might involve him in endless difficulties with next of kin; that no sort of national public health or welfare authorities existed so that the cleansing and maintenance of waterways, streets, towns depended on the energy or whim of provincial officials, and that in consequence there was not one really good stretch of road anywhere in the Empire.

China's pre-industrial economic, military and social organisation had already resulted in its being twice defeated by Western powers since the century began – by the British in the Opium Wars of the 1840s and by the Anglo-French Expeditionary Forces of 1858 and 1860. These conflicts, which succeeded in their aim of forcing the Chinese to open a number of their ports to foreign trade and residence, also increased Chinese suspicion and fear of the West which resulted in an inward-looking, reactionary xenophobia that remained a dominating strain in the country for the rest of the century. However, running counter to this, there developed a 'self-strengthening movement' among certain sections of the educated classes who recognised that China had to come to terms with the pressing modern world.

One of the early 'self-strengtheners' was a scholar named Feng Kuei-Fen who wrote about his sense of personal humiliation and outrage at the result of the Anglo-French expeditions. The hats of 'all who are conscious in their minds and have spirit in their blood' must, he declared, 'be raised by their hair standing on end . . . because the largest country on the globe . . . is yet controlled by small barbarians'. 'Why are we large yet weak?' he demanded. 'Why are they small and yet strong?'

Those were big questions. One of the more obvious answers was China's lack of modern armaments and systems of communication, which was the point forcibly made by another 'self-strengthener', Tso Tsung-t'ang, when he submitted 'Tso's Plan' to the government for consideration. Tso was Governor-General of Chekiang and his proposal was for the development of a shipyard at Fuchou where efficient Western-style steamships could be built. Tso was worried about the activities of the Japanese who, he said, had already bought a steamship from England and then taken it apart 'for examination and imitation'. Both Japan and China, he pointed out, saw the potential of the high seas, but 'Japan has something to rely upon and we have nothing. It is like crossing a river where others are rowing a boat while we are making a raft. It is like racing, when others are riding on a steed while we are riding on a donkey. How is this possible? All of us are human beings whose intelligence and wisdom are by nature similar, but in practice we cannot help being different. Chinese wisdom is spent on abstract things; the foreigners' intelligence is concentrated upon concrete things. The Chinese take the principles of the classics as a foundation and mechanical matters as the practical details; foreigners consider mechanical matters important, principles unimportant. Each of the two believes what it thinks right and neither can understand the other . . .'

This view of China's position in the world, written by a China-man in 1866, was fairly common currency among Westerners. It was the cliché image of West facing East: on the one side, the hustling man of action, not too hot on philosophy or culture but a dab hand at making things work, which was what counted when the crunches came; on the other, the poor old donkey-back, head-in-the-classics Oriental in his land of 'eternal standstill' who assumed that any raft was stout enough for the oceans of the world.

Like most clichés it was rather less than a half-truth and knobbed with contradictions. For instance, many of China's technical pro-cesses had been far ahead of the West's until the end of the Middle Ages and many of its people were very practical and down to earth in their fashion. Also, all Westerners were not so untroubled by matters of philosophy and principle, and yet those Westerners who were generally most disliked and distrusted by the Chinese were precisely the ones most concerned with such matters. Missionaries, at least the thoughtful among them, were the first to surmise that the introduction of modern technology to China without any accompanying social and administrative reorganisa-tion might have violent results. And so it did, but one of the great missionary mistakes was the assumption that the Chinese needed Christianity as much as they needed steamships. The Western package deal of merchants, plus diplomats, plus missionaries, seemed to be succeeding fairly well in Africa, India and the South Seas, so why wasn't it right for China?

Christian missionaries, a persistent and restive company, had been trying to push their part of the deal upon the Chinese ever since the late sixteenth century, when Matteo Ricci and his fellow Jesuits reached China and for a few years were actually allowed to live in Peking. During the seventeenth century, French, Portu-guese, Spanish and Italian missionaries of the Dominican, Francis-can and Jesuit Orders consolidated the hold of the Catholic Church and a Chinese bishop was appointed by the Pope to the See of Nanking in 1690, by which time the missionaries claimed to have made about three hundred thousand converts. However, bitter disputes arose among the various Orders, and between them and their superiors in Europe, over the tricky question of accommodating the universal Chinese practice of ancestor worship to Christianity. The ensuing Rites Controversy lasted for nearly a century and in 1773, partly as a result of it, the Society of Jesus, whose members had been at the forefront of Christian infiltration in the Far East, was disbanded by order of the Pope and there followed a period of persecution in China during which missionaries and their converts were exiled, imprisoned or killed. The later Emperors of the Manchu dynasty, that had begun in 1644, adopted an increasingly hostile, exclusive policy towards all Westerners and their religion until, in the eighteenth century, imperial edicts forbidding Christian worship were issued and all rights of foreign trade and residence were confined to the southern port of Canton.

It was thus Canton which became the first centre of the Protestant mission movement in China and its founding father was a young Scotsman, Robert Morrison of the London Missionary Society. Morrison reached Canton in 1807 and stayed there for twenty-seven years during which he brought out the first Chinese version of the Bible and converted just ten Chinamen. It was hardly a success story, but Morrison struck the fittingly valiant note with his answer to the incredulous question of whether he really expected to convert the Chinese single-handed: 'No, but I expect God can.' The reply was indicative of the Protestants' general approach. They knew that the obstacles and problems in the way of China's Christianisation were almost overwhelmingly formidable in human terms, but these never really deterred them because they were certain of eventual success in accordance with the Divine Will.

Morrison was soon joined at Canton by some other missionaries who felt a special call to the unyielding Celestial Empire. His first colleague from the LMS was William Milne, who at once set about 'acquiring the Chinese', a task he feelingly characterised for generations of future evangelists without the gift of tongues as one for men 'with bodies of brass, lungs of steel, heads of oak, hands of spring-steel, eyes of eagles, hearts of apostles, memories of angels and lives of Methuselah'. The first American missionaries to China, Elijah C. Bridgman and David Abeel of the American Board of Commissioners for Foreign Missions (mercifully abbreviated to 'The Board' or the ABCFM) reached Canton in 1830 and were followed by other compatriots – Dr Peter Parker, the first medical missionary to open a hospital in China, and Samuel Wells Williams who wrote by far the most delightful of all the early attempts to explain China to the West entitled *The Middle Kingdom, its geography, government, education, social life, arts, religion, etc; and its inhabitants.*

The maverick missionary of this early period, of which each generation bred a small stock, was Karl Friedrich Gutzlaff, a Pomeranian with, according to one who knew him, 'an intolerable assumption of omniscience'. Because missionaries were not allowed to travel beyond Canton, Gutzlaff took a job as interpreter on Jardine Matheson's opium-carrying ships in order to disseminate his Christian tracts widely, which was a classic case of the inattentive right hand. He also employed the first Chinese colporteurs, men who sold Bibles and preached in areas where foreigners were unwelcome or positively excluded. The idea was used by other societies and during the 1840s and 50s the British and Foreign Bible Society arranged for the printing of more than a quarter of a million Chinese New Testaments. But it proved impossible to distribute them in a satisfactory and meaningful way because there were insufficient missionaries for the work and the colporteurs frequently proved men of straw who sold the Bibles profitably for their paper value alone and then concocted dreamy figures about the conversions they had made. Gutzlaff's colporteurs were guilty of this and the uncovering of their deception ruined his already somewhat ambiguous reputation. The Chinese Evangelisation Society, under whose auspices Hudson Taylor first went to China, was an offshoot of Gutzlaff's proselytising zeal and knowledge of this might have cheered him up; but by the time Taylor returned to the country as leader of the China Inland Mission, Gutzlaff was dead and his evangelisation society defunct.

The Netherlands Missionary Society that first supported Gutzlaff was the second arrival in the Chinese field, but it did not flourish like the pioneering LMS, all of whose early members showed great initiative. Another famous man among them was Dr James Legge who reached Canton in 1843 and made it his life's work to 'open the door to the mind of the Chinese' by translating the Chinese classics into English. His labours ran into sixty-six volumes and were the most influential and authoritative versions for many years. Legge possessed an unusually sympathetic understanding of the native philosophers, nevertheless he regretfully decided that Confucius 'threw no new light on any of the questions which have a world-wide interest. He gave no impulse to religion. He had no sympathy with progress. His influence has been wonderful, but it will henceforth wane . . .'

Most of the missionaries had much less respect than that for the Chinese sages and were outspoken in their condemnation of China's intellectual and moral life. 'There is nothing to be seen all over the land but the widespread indications of spiritual death,' wrote William Muirhead, a contemporary and colleague of Legge's. The 'torpidity and immobility of the Chinese mind' made him shudder; how could one force such people 'to see the necessity of progress'? Especially when, adding insult to apathy, they had such mistakenly 'high and overweening ideas of themselves as a nation and a culture'.

That his ideas of his own culture were equally 'overweening' did not occur to Mr Muirhead nor to many of his fellow missionaries; but it was nevertheless true that the Chinese had for long been totally convinced of the rightness and indisputable superiority of their ancient civilisation. This obtained in the religious sphere as in all others and any new faith introduced from abroad was first labelled a heterodoxy – Buddhism, when it reached China about the first century AD, was termed a 'barbarian miasma'. Thus the whole tradition of orthodox, inward-looking Chinese thought flowed against any easy acceptance of Christianity, as did the natural conservatism of the masses and their relative disinterest in metaphysical abstractions. It was, in short, a gloomier outlook than the early Protestant missionaries fully realised when they went striding optimistically in, determined to achieve the humanly impossible.

While missionaries grieved over the moral and spiritual short-comings of the Chinese, other Westerners were ever ready to make lists of all the modern conveniences and appurtenances China lacked. One of the great merchant mistakes was to assume that the people would buy up massive quantities of Manchester textile goods, lamps, locomotives and bottled beer if only they could afford them. In the event the one really profitable foreign import proved to be opium and it was this situation that opened the whole question of foreign trading rights and concessions in China and led to the tragi-farce of the Opium Wars (1840–2) and the opening of the first five 'treaty ports', Amoy, Canton, Fuchou, Shanghai and Ningpo. Within the port limits as designated by treaty agreements, foreigners could reside and pursue their trade, whether it was the continuing import of opium or the spreading of the gospel message; they also enjoyed the right of extra-territoriality, which meant that they were not subject to Chinese jurisdiction but to the law as administered by their own consular representatives.

Among the first Protestant missionaries to establish centres in these newly opened ports were members of the Church Mission-ary Society, who went to Shanghai and Ningpo in 1844. The CMS was the missionary branch of the evangelical movement. It was a movement both practical and philanthropic which cut across traditional sectarian divisions in Britain and America and was the chief stimulus for the initiation and growth of most of the Protest-ant missionary societies that were founded in the late eighteenth century.

It is difficult, these days, to make a committed, dyed-in-the-wool Evangelical sound attractive. From the accounts of the Society for the Prevention of Vice launched by the first great evangelical leader, William Wilberforce, through the prolifera-tion of societies set up in the early nineteenth century, some to provide relief for the poor (there really *was* a Forlorn Females Fund of Mercy), others to make sure the poor didn't actually enjoy themselves (there was also a Society for Promoting the

Closure of Sunday Fairs), and on to the jocular self-confidence of the great revivalist preachers who, as one sceptic put it, always 'approached the burning bush with cheerful aplomb', and the later hardening of that joy into a spirit which was increasingly exclusive and self-righteous, the epithets attached to the noun Evangelical are usually these: pious, narrow, high-minded, smug, prim, morbid. Even the evangelical virtues – chastity, zeal, charity, probity – are not fashionable nowadays.

Evangelicism centred its morality on the practical simple virtues of Victorian home life and tended to run very much in families. Playing the let's-pretend-we're-in-church game so popular in evangelical nurseries, big brother, wearing his pinnie as a surplice, took up an elevated position on his desk and exhorted his unre-deemed younger siblings to the paths of righteousness. Sometimes there must have been considerable competition for the 'pulpit' – in the Devonshire home of Reverend Henry Moule, for instance, three of whose sons later took holy orders. The best known among them was the evangelical Bishop Handley Moule of Cambridge, then there was George, who went to China as a CMS missionary in 1858, and lastly, because younger, there was Arthur Evans Moule.

Arthur's early career was typecast: Cambridge of course and peaceful vacations spent fly-fishing and water-colouring, followed by CMS theological college in Islington, London; he was there at the time of the Indian Mutiny and offered himself at once for the Indian field, fired by the devout young man's ardour for martyrdom. However, after ordination he decided to follow his brother George instead and sailed for China in 1860 with his new wife, a missionary's daughter, Eliza Agnes. Their ages, for fledgling missionaries, were quite typical: Arthur was twenty-five, Eliza, nineteen. They travelled by the 'all-blue-water' route, which meant they saw no land for eighty-four days between England and Java Head. On eventual arrival they went directly to Ningpo where George and his wife lived in a mission house near the Fairy Bridge; bundles of decomposing cats always hung under the bridge because the Chinese knew that the ghost of any decently buried, unhung feline prowled at night.

It was a troublous time to reach China. Those Anglo-French Expeditions had just forced the Chinese to open eleven more treaty ports, three of them on the River Yangtze, as agreed in the 1860 Treaty of Peking. From the missionary point of view, Article 29 of the Treaty was the most significant. It stated that 'the principles of the Christian religion as professed by the Protestant and Roman Catholic churches are recognised as teaching men to do good and do to others as they would have others do to them. Hereafter, those who quietly teach and profess these doctrines shall not be harassed or persecuted on account of their faith.' It went on to say that any who taught and/or practised Christianity, be they Chinese or foreign, should not be 'interfered with or molested', and the implication was that, if the Chinese government failed to give Christians sufficient protection from any persecution, Western powers would be justified in taking action.

At the same time that the Chinese were trying to fend off the military-backed demands of the major Western powers, their imperial forces were also trying to cope with the civil rebellion of the Taipings, who were beginning to create bloody chaos in and around Ningpo, the 'City of the Peaceful Wave', just about the time that Arthur and Eliza Moule arrived there. When the rebellion began, in the previous decade, several British and American missionaries tried to make fruitful contact with the Taiping leader, Hung Hsiu-ch'uan, who claimed to have had mystical religious experiences on Christian themes. These had apparently resulted from his earnest study of tracts given to him by a convert of Robert Morrison's and of Gutzlaff's attempted translation of the Bible. The missionaries were hopeful therefore that Hung would become the founder of an indigenous Christian movement and several times braved the insurgents' territory in order to talk with the rebel leaders. Two young LMS missionaries, Joseph Edkins and Griffith John, both with active and distinguished careers ahead of them, were the first to do this. They presented Bibles to the Taiping 'Kings' in Suchou and later reported that, in their view, 'the religious element enters very powerfully into this great revolutionary movement. Nothing can be more erroneous than to suppose it is a purely political one.'

Certainly it was true that the Taiping leaders had been greatly influenced by Christianity. They believed in one God, called all foreigners their 'brethren of the western oceans' and encouraged their troops to loot and destroy native temples. ('I saw many a statue with its arm or head chopped off by a playful Taiping,' commented Arthur Moule, hinting it was a game in which he would quite like to have joined.) Iconoclasm of this sort was allowable, but Hung was also a visionary to whose head power soon went. He convinced himself that he was none other than the younger brother of Jesus Christ with a divinely-inspired commission to overthrow the Manchu dynasty and establish the 'Heavenly Kingdom of Great Peace' in China. This was, of course, outrageous heresy to every right-thinking missionary, and those who, like Edkins and John, had earlier pleaded the rebel cause, were disillusioned. As time went on the Taiping leaders became increasingly brutal, fanatical and dissolute and totally discredited the movement in foreign eyes.

Not that this halted the rebellion, for throughout the 1850s and early 60s bands of Taipings, made up of impoverished peasants, unemployed boatmen, unsuccessful beggars, pirates, army deserters – the 'offscourings of many provinces' Arthur Moule termed them – continued to rampage and ravage the land, meeting only sporadic resistance from the government's forces. In the winter of 1861, while Arthur was struggling for mastery of the Chinese language and Eliza was awaiting the birth of her first child, the rebels converged upon Ningpo.

Civil revolts in China seem always to have certain common characteristics: they go on for an inordinately long time, they falter, re-shape, spatter into bursts of extreme brutality, and are often such an inconclusive muddle that even those on the spot can give no very coherent account of them afterwards. Thus the Taipings plagued Ningpo intermittently for eighteen months and Arthur Moule, there the whole time, found that even the townspeople seldom knew what was happening. In October 1861 he and George were itinerating through the neighbouring countryside watching the peasant women peacefully plucking the red and yellow globes in the persimmon orchards; a month later those same peasants had merged into pathetic huddles of homeless refugees who trailed first into Ningpo and then fled on towards the coast.

The Moules stayed, though Arthur's Chinese 'pundit' shook in his chair at the sound of distant muskets crackling, and the city walls bristled with wooden beams and iron spikes ready to shove down upon the invaders. But on 7th December the Taipings, holding mats aloft to protect their heads from the descending wood and iron, attacked and took the native city in a few hours. The British and American missionaries had already been evacuated to the International Settlement on the opposite river bank, which was not molested owing to the presence of Western gunboats on the intervening waters. So Arthur and George played hockey with British and French naval officers on the ice-covered moat near the city's Salt Gate that Christmastide and helped to decorate the wardrooms with holly. In the spring those same gunboats helped the Imperial Forces to recapture Ningpo from the rebels, in the course of which conflict two cannon-balls from HMS *Encounter* were accidentally tossed on the verandah of the CMS mission house. The Moules treasured them as mementoes and were wise to do so, for, as the years went by and their hair turned grey 'in China's service', a prestigious rarity value was conferred upon any Westerner who could claim to have been within a cannon's shot of the Taiping Rebellion.

The rebels returned briefly to Ningpo the following year and soon after their second retreat found themselves faced with the government's Ever Victorious Army commanded by the formidable 'British Gordon'. At long last in 1864 the revolt was crushed; Hung committed suicide in shame, having failed his 'elder brother's' expectations; General Gordon became 'Chinese Gordon', hero of the British press and single-handed slaughterer of the terrible Taipings. In Ningpo it was suggested that a monument be raised in memory of the 'gallant British and French marines who had died to save the city', as Arthur put it. But its proposed aggressive and loftily phallus-shaped design offended the local citizenry, who said it would disturb the spirits of the neighbouring air. So the foreign community had to settle for a very small square obelisk, a typical example, Moule complained, 'of Chinese ingratitude'.

By the time peace was restored, Arthur had become a fairly competent Chinese linguist and he could read that the druggist next door was called 'The Double-Headed Phoenix' and that a nearby poster announced the coming of a Nanking acting troupe to the tea-gardens of the Crimson Oleander on the western hill. It was time for him to stand alone while George pushed outwards to Hangchow, a riverine city about equidistant from Shanghai and Ningpo.

Once the imperial capital and with a long-cherished reputation for beauty, culture and sensuality, Hangchow had been fearfully decimated by the Taipings. 'Famine, the sword and hardship of every conceivable kind have conspired to destroy these wretched people,' George wrote on arrival there in the winter of 1864. So few citizens were left that he was able to rent a house with unusual ease and could thus claim the distinction of being the first Protestant missionary to establish a definite residential mission inland.

The mission was detached and secluded behind high mud walls, with accommodation on the second storey for George and his growing family and rooms for a native catechist and a chapel on the ground floor. It was a splendid find but a wee bit isolated from the main stream of potential converts, so George also rented a half-wrecked fanmaker's shop in a busy thoroughfare to use as a street chapel. Most missionaries had street chapels, often named 'Good News Halls' in Chinese, which were open to all comers. They were equipped with a few rough wooden benches, a raised dais, texts on the white-washed walls, a table loaded with tracts at the door, and a blackboard on which was chalked the theme of the next sermon. The oddity of such places and their schoolroom atmosphere attracted the people with their natural curiosity and regard for learning, and George usually had an audience for his daily sermons. But neither this method nor the itinerations in which Arthur specialised produced much in the way of results. 'I visited in all during the months of March, May, October, November and December, seventy-one places large and small,' Arthur wrote home. 'One of these I visited five times, four of them four, six of them three, twenty-one on two occasions and the remainder once . . . One precious fruit has, I trust, resulted from this work – an old woman baptized on 18th December. She heard the gospel in a neighbouring village last May . . .' Not that Arthur was especially ineffectual, for his experience was typical of the many meagre rewards Protestant missionaries gleaned during the 60s. Their annual reports showed very few true conversions and led George Morrison, the *Times* correspondent, to conclude later that 'their harvest may be described as amounting to a fraction more than two Chinamen per missionary per annum'.

Considering the numerousness of the Chinese and the fact that, in the 1860s, there were only about ninety Protestant missionaries in the entire country, there should have been plenty of preaching room for any who cared to take up China's challenge and plenty of fraternal sympathy for untried methods and ideas. But missionaries had always been on the defensive in the Celestial Empire and the erosions of doubt, dislike, disinterest, failure and ridicule did not strengthen them. They tended to carp and snarl, to jealously guard each small 'fruit' they found, to fear in every newcomer to the field, a potentially more successful rival.

various refinements such as well-kept public gardens, well-lit carriage roads, well-dressed idle ladies that helped to justify its later boast as the 'Model Settlement' of the Far East. A week or so before the arrival of the CIM party, the foreigners had added the attraction of a cross-country paperchase on horseback to its growing Sport and Recreational Calendar. While in full cry, riders had trampled over a few paddies behind the town and some of the hounds got a whiff of hare which they finally ran to earth in an ancestral graveyard, digging up a corpse in the process. But if the Chinese *would* refuse to fence their fields properly or bury their dead deeply, what else could they expect, as the paperchasers asked each other through the columns of the local newspaper?

The *Lammermuir* party too proved fair game for the press, especially when they all donned Chinese dress for the first time. This practice was one that Taylor was passionately determined upon when he formed his own independent mission, and the letter in which he set out his reasons for it is cogent: 'I am not alone in the opinion that the foreign dress and carriage of missionaries . . . the foreign appearance of chapels and indeed the foreign air imparted to everything connected with their work has seriously hindered the rapid dissemination of the Truth among the Chinese. And why should such a foreign aspect be given to Christianity? The Word of God does not require it, nor I conceive, could sound reason justify it. It is not the de-nationalization but the Christianisation of this people that we seek. We wish to see Chinese Christians raised up – men and women truly Christian but withal truly Chinese in the right sense of the word. We wish to see churches of such believers presided over by pastors and officers of their own country, worshipping God in the land of their fathers and in their own tongue and in edifices of a thoroughly native style of architecture. "It is enough that the disciple be as his Master." If we really wish to see the Chinese as we have described, let us as far as possible set before them a true example. Let us in everything not sinful become Chinese that we may by all means "save some". Let us adopt their dress, acquire their language, seek to conform to their habits and approximate to their diet as far as health and constitution will allow. Let us live in their houses, making no unnecessary alterations in external form and only so far modifying their internal arrangements as efficiency for work absolutely requires.' This, Taylor concluded, 'cannot but involve a certain measure of inconvenience', but would any who reflected upon the sacrificial and self-denying life of Jesus himself 'hesitate to make such trifling sacrifices for His Name'?

Taylor's recognition that, firstly, the Christianity being disseminated in China *was* Western-style, with all its Anglican, Methodist or Roman trappings intact and, secondly, that there *was* a wide and mutually inhibiting cultural gap between Chinaman and missionary, put his thinking about a generation ahead of most of his Protestant colleagues. Stiff-necked Taylor certainly was when it came to the dispensations of the Divine Grace, but many of his ideas on method were far-sighted and enterprising. Thus, just before his party left Shanghai for the interior, the men put on long loose Chinese robes, had their heads shaved in front and false pigtails woven into their back hair; the women coiled their hair in simple buns and also put on native gowns – which must have been a great relief after whale-bone tight lacing. They could not, of course, cram their feet into the four-inch-long shoes worn by the foot-bound Chinese women, nor could the men disguise their heavier, hairier bodies; in any case, as Taylor realised, 'merely to put on Chinese dress and act regardless of their thoughts and feelings is to make a burlesque of the whole matter'.

The CIM adoption of native dress was neither a disguise nor a parody, but a gracious gesture of conciliation and one which, after a time, individualistic members of other societies also tried. One of them was Timothy Richard, the well-known Baptist missionary, who, on the very first afternoon that he donned native robes, was invited into a home to drink tea. 'I understood then,' he wrote, 'that there had been a sound reason for not asking me before. In foreign dress I would have been such a strange sight that all sorts of onlookers would have come to the paper window, noiselessly made a hole in the paper with a wet fingertip and applied an eye to it. My every visit to the house would have thus involved the replacement of a window pane. But when the foreigner put on Chinese dress he was much like an ordinary

Chinaman and not worth looking at.' This and other similar incidents convinced Richard that wearing native dress helped to break down social barriers and he habitually wore it throughout his distinguished and active career. But this sort of reasoning did not impress the foreign settlers in Shanghai – most of whom had no desire to drink tea in a native home anyway – and when the *Lammermuir* party left the port *à la chinoise* the local smart set hooted with derision.

They went first by river to Hangchow, that former imperial capital. Proud relics like the pagodas of the Six Harmonies and the Thundering Peak still spiked the city's sky-line; frogs croaked among the ruins of the Sung Dynasty pleasure-gardens; autumnal sea mist, seeping inland, hung all day among the exposed white roots of the mulberry trees along the riverbanks. The river itself, main thoroughfare to the city, supported the invariable Chinese jumble of flat-bottomed junks and flimsy scudding cockles; 'slipper-boats' closed at the 'toe' and open at the 'heel' where the rowers stood and one-man 'foot-boats' with sculls that were propelled with the naked foot; leaky rafts, some topped with sheltering bamboo tunnels, and trading boats loaded with oil, pork, firewood, fish or flowers. The walls of the city, girt with walls wide enough for six men to walk along abreast, were pierced by six gates. As the sun went down each night, the gate-guards lit a red candle and placed it in a socket in the ground, where it flickered for about twenty minutes. When the flame sputtered out a gong sounded and all the gates slammed shut till dawn – though there were, apparently, unofficial and precarious ways in via rope and basket. Around the gates leprous verminous beggars scratched and starved; the gates of the central yamen (official residence of the district governor) were emblazoned with inscriptions announcing the cherishing, protecting, improving and purifying characteristics of he who dwelt within; in the secluded houses of the wealthy, also protected by gates and keepers, chalky powdered women in violet or sea-green satins lolled, gossiped, gazed languidly out of semi-transparent windows made from scraped shells. It was in a house of that type near the Periwinkle Gate that George Moule of the CMS lived with his wife and children, his native catechists and assistants, his cook, head boy, chapel keeper and courtyard sweeper.

The conflict that resulted from the unplanned and undesired proximity of these two pioneering missionary groups was precedent and prototype of the sort of schisms that were to rack the whole Protestant movement in China for the rest of the century. On the one side, scholarly, courteous, cultured Reverend George Moule of the Anglican Church, he and his wife from distinguished clerical-missionary families; on the other, the tense fanatical son of the Barnsley chemist with his narrow passion for souls, his utter certainty of divine direction, and his assorted, untrained party of pregnant wife, children, blacksmiths, carpenters, unattached spinsters and so on. The divisions between the two were doctrinal, temperamental, denominational and social, and proved too deep to be bridged by the bond of common purpose that should have united them.

The CIM group found shelter in a dilapidated, dirt-encrusted rabbit-warren of a building through which blasted the winter gales. On its bare floors they dumped the invariable missionary-muddle of prayer-books, clothes, medicines, tracts, tins of Epps cocoa, photographs of mother and father, nappies, bottles of Blackwood's ink. They slept on wooden frame beds strung with coarse fibre and ate their meals in a bare hall on a plank table set with bowls and chopsticks; on the wall their first Chinese text was displayed, 'Even Christ pleased not Himself'. To some of them, nevertheless, great pleasure soon came, in the learning of the language, the organizing of the household, the singing of hymns and the holding of their first Sunday services, which the people attended in fairly large, if undiscriminating numbers. 'You would be amused at many things we see,' Jennie Faulding wrote to her parents. 'A man nursing an immense dog all through the service, a woman mending a man's shoe and a mother close by giving me a lesson in the approved style of dressing her child's hair, using her thin fingers as a comb . . . It is so nice,' she concluded, 'to be just where I am and to have the work that I have . . . Such a wide field and I feel so free and happy in it . . .'

The Chinese dubbed Jennie 'Miss Happiness' because, for the

first time in her life, she had found an acceptable, challenging outlet for her natural energy and enthusiasm; some other members of the mission, whose basic motivations had been very different from the beginning, found their situation much less satisfactory. Chief malcontent was Lewis Nicol whose Chinese gowns made him feel humiliated and vulnerable and, he decided, lowered his standing in the eyes of the natives and exposed him to the ridicule of other Westerners. As he had assumed that the status of a gentleman was automatically conferred by the missionary vocation, the latter aspect was perhaps the more galling. In an effort to avoid a row, Taylor sent Nicol and his wife to start an 'out-station' in a town ten miles from Hangchow, but once there the renegades put their Western clothes back on and began using knives and forks. Their outlandish ways and generally overbearing behaviour were too much for the local district officer who had them forcibly ejected and sent back to Hangchow.

Shaken but unrepentant, Nicol turned for support to George Moule, who was, after all, a gentleman mindful of maintaining his superior position in relation to the orientals, as, at home, he kept a proper distance from the labouring classes. The alliance between the two men was thus particularly unseemly and Moule must have thoroughly hated and distrusted Taylor to credit the very nasty things that Nicol had to say about his leader. Taylor, Nicol suggested, was not only a petty dictator and a crank, but he had far too many unattached females about his household. Exactly what he said is unknown, but he plainly insinuated that Hudson was keeping a sort of Hangchow harem with at least two mistresses in addition to his wife.

Moule lapped it up and expressed the opinion in letters home that the China Inland Mission was a 'sham and a delusion'; moreover it was scarcely proper for so many 'young unmarried ladies' to be in the mission at all, much less living in Taylor's home and apparently receiving a goodnight kiss from their leader before going to bed. Brimming with righteousness, Moule also wrote to Taylor in terms of unctuous hostility: 'Consider I beg you what hazard your own soul runs in this connection. You are their physician and spiritual pastor and live in close proximity, with some of the restraints of social etiquette relaxed.' In such perilous circumstances, he continued, 'you would be more than human if you were not capable of being tempted to lay aside in some measure the reserve with which they, for their sakes and your own, ought to be treated . . .' Finally Moule, speaking as one who 'for twenty years has known a plague in my own breast', strongly advised Taylor to 'put a speedy end' to the whole CIM so that 'further perils may be averted'.

By this time Nicol had three other adherents among the group, but the rest remained loyal to Taylor and some – Jennie Faulding, Emily Blatchley, George Duncan (the stonemason), Will Rudland – staunchly defended him. Hudson himself was harrowed by this early betrayal of the mission's first principles and the insinuations about his sexual behaviour shocked him profoundly. His only recourse, Emily Blatchley recorded, was to ask Williamson (the carpenter) 'to receive from each of us ladies individually a statement as to Mr Taylor's bearing towards us being nothing but that of a Christian and a gentleman. I rebelled, revolted at his having to stoop so – as if his character were even on an impeachable level, but he thinks it better to condescend to unquestionable proof for the mission's sake and from each of us Mr Williamson received the required testimony . . .' Emily was hurt as much as anyone by the silly affair, for she was devoted to both the Taylors. 'God is stronger than Moule,' she announced with furious underlinings in her secret journal, and 'Moule seems to ignore *Mrs Taylor's existence*'.

Maria Taylor, who had just given birth to a daughter in very trying circumstances and who knew the accusations were groundless, had her own interpretation of their troubles: 'We have come to fight Satan in his very stronghold and he will not let us alone,' she wrote to friends. 'One sometimes feels almost overwhelmed with the sense of Satan's power here; but our God will not forsake us . . . One is almost tempted to ask, "Why was Mr Nicol permitted to come out?" Perhaps it was that our mission might be thoroughly established on a right basis early in its history . . .' Maria had the unfailing ability to interpret all misfortunes and difficulties in one of two ways: either they were sure evidence that

God was testing the moral fibre of the little band or, if the disasters were too severe to have been instigated by an essentially merciful Power, then they were the work of Satan – and therefore proof positive that the group was working on the right lines because the Devil himself was trying to hinder it.

For several months Satan kept up the attack. George Moule went home on furlough, satisfied with what Taylor termed his 'consummate piece of priestly presumption' and Arthur took up his brother's cudgels. He had several stormy meetings with Taylor and once, the latter recorded, 'he told me that I had brought out persons who had more need to be beside someone who was able to teach them English grammar and manners than to be teaching the Chinese Christianity'. The tensions and anxieties sharpened to knife-edge the intensity of Taylor's spiritual life. He could not rest in Maria's certainties but had to go deeply tunnelling for his own. 'I felt assured that there was in Christ all I needed, but the practical question was – how to get it out,' was how he tried to describe his state of mind at this time. And, 'I knew full well that there was in the root, the stem, abundant fatness, but how to get it into my puny little branch was the question.'

On the practical level too Taylor pushed himself remorselessly, 'planting' his trusted recruits in out-stations, preaching and ministering in the little dispensary that he had opened at the Hangchow mission. Though Jennie and Emily continued to live in the mission household, Taylor kept a cooler distance from them and there were no more goodnight kisses. 'I am so lonely, so utterly alone,' Emily wrote in her journal. 'And now my intercourse with them (Hudson and Maria) must be straitened even yet more. But why should I cling so? Oh Christ, take hold of my hands . . . I find such joy in being with the Taylors, but I must not let it intoxicate me. I must not revel in it . . .'

Thus lonely, tubercular, highly-strung little Emily wrote up her journal with a blunt pencil in her frigid Hangchow bedroom in February 1867. For desk, a tin trunk covered with an antimacassar, a bamboo stool for a seat; there was a zinc bath and a chamber-pot under the truckle bed, an oil lamp and photographs on her bedside table and, on the one shelf, her Bible, prayer-book, a torn copy of the *Regent's Park Monthly Messenger*, a pair of stockings the rats had nibbled, and a bright homely packet of gingerbread nuts from 'Jennie dearie' whose parents sent regular supplies of goodies. In the next room, similar but equipped with a few more comforts, Jennie described the pattern of her days to her mother. 'It's eight o'clock breakfast, reading a lesson till nine, then prayers, then my Hangchow teacher comes and we change hymns from the Ningpo to the Hangchow dialect and do half an hour of writing the character. 12.30 prayers and then dinner and after it I am with the women till six. Then tea and prayers and housekeeping accounts and another hour of the character until bed . . .'

So by the spring the loyal members of the group had fashioned working routines and rituals which gave them anchorage in the chaotic and profane city; Hudson, meanwhile, continued to expand their 'field of operations'. George Duncan was sent to Nanking where, ironically, the only person who would grant him accommodation was the Buddhist priest who kept the famous Drum Tower. Duncan, the only foreigner in the city, lived in the tower for several months, walking the streets handing out tracts by day and sleeping in the Tower – during the intervals between the drum's great boom. He left no written record of this unique experience because he was, in the gentle missionary language, 'not specially gifted or cultured', but a 'stalwart Highlander' possessed of great grit and perseverance – a man in the frontier tradition. Thirty-five years later, Taylor, speaking with the usual wistful nostalgia of the pioneer for the wholesome, straightforward early days, made the interesting admission that many of his first recruits 'were humble people. If they were to offer to our Mission now they might not be accepted – George Duncan for example . . .', who, nevertheless, was one 'willing to live anywhere and endure anything if only souls might be saved'.

While Hudson was away settling his workers in strategic, uncomfortable locations, Maria calmly reigned in Hangchow, organising bible and sewing classes among 'the women', looking after the household and her five children. The eldest, a 'little maid of eight and a half', survives in the annals of the CIM as a classic example of the Victorian child-saint, and stories such as this are told about her in Taylor's biography: once, out walking with her father, 'little Gracie noticed a man making an idol. "Oh Papa," she said earnestly, "he doesn't know about Jesus or he would never do it! Won't you tell him?"' Her hand clasped in his, Mr Taylor did so, the child following his words with eager interest. Further on they sat down 'to rest in a shady place' and Taylor suggested she should pray for the man. 'She did so and never had I heard such a prayer,' Taylor wrote. 'She had seen the man making an idol; her heart was full and the dear child was talking to God on his behalf.'

A week after this incident Gracie suddenly died of hydrocephalus, and parents, siblings, friends gathered round her couch in a juvenile deathbed tableau worthy of inclusion in any number of *The Sunday Scholar's Friend* or *The Child's Visitor and Pleasing Instructor*. 'I think I never saw anything so perfect as the remains of that dear child,' Hudson wrote home, his agonised grief not the less real for its literary overtones. 'The long silken eyelashes under the finely arched brows, nose so delicately chiselled, mouth small and sweetly expressive, the purity of the white features, the quiet composure of the countenance – all are deeply impressed on heart and memory. In her sweet little Chinese jacket and little hands folded on her bosom holding a single flower – oh it was passing fair and so hard to close forever from our sight!'

Gracie's was a 'good death' because, as the missionaries half-acknowledged to themselves, they found it full of meaning – the necessary sacrifice of the purest and most innocent lamb to the jealous God of Love. Gracie's very perfection doomed her: 'I am thankful she was taken rather than any of the others, though she was the sunshine of our lives,' Taylor wrote. People so ardently sustained by faith were enviably equipped to cope with sudden death and one that seemed as significant and seraphic as Gracie's brought them a renewal of strength and unity. 'He is keeping Satan altogether under just now,' Emily Blatchley wrote soon after it. 'How grateful we ought to feel for the state of things in the mission now as compared with a few months ago – when our lute seemed too full of rifts for harmony ever to come back again.' The splinter group headed by Lewis Nicol finally left the mission

1   The *Lammermuir* party: (*from left to right*) *seated, 2nd,* William Rudland, *3rd and 4th,* Mr and Mrs Lewis Nicol, *5th,* Jennie Faulding, *6th and 7th,* Hudson and Maria Taylor; *standing, 4th,* Emily Blatchley, *5th,* George Duncan

2 Arthur Moule, Archdeacon of Mid-China

3 George Moule, Bishop of Mid-China

4   Hudson Taylor with his children and his second wife, Jennie Faulding (*right*), and Emily Blatchley (*left*) and a Chinese servant (Howard Taylor is standing between his stepmother and Miss Blatchley)

5   Dr and Mrs Timothy Richard

6   A colporteur boarding a boat to offer books

that autumn and the dispute between the Moules and the Taylors damped to a cold silence. But what a deplorable spectacle it had been – the only two groups of English missionaries resident outside the treaty ports quarrelling over the use of knife or chopstick, 'taking testimonies' about one man's sexual propriety and sneering about another man's grammar. But major issues were involved which rankled long, and that was only the first of many occasions when emotive phrases about the 'proper conduct for young unmarried ladies', the 'presumptions of priests', and the dangers of 'going native' were to be bandied around missionary circles.

CHAPTER FOUR

Riot

The CIM pioneers set another precedent of conflict which was to be frequently re-enacted during the rest of the century. The back-drop this time was the city of Yangchow, the time, summer of the following year. By then several more recruits had arrived from England and, in April, Taylor decided to leave a nucleus of experienced workers at Hangchow while he and his family, Emily Blatchley and six Chinese evangelists moved further into the yearned-for interior. Rivers were the main roads of nineteenth-century China, so the party again travelled by houseboat – a journey of some four hundred miles that took several weeks.

Compared to most missionaries, CIM members said very little about the physical scene, for their writings are characterised by an intense concentration on the state of their personal spiritual relationship with God and continual laments at the unredeemed state of the people around them. During this long boat journey however, they did unbutton themselves sufficiently to enjoy the welcome of the spring. It was, conventionally, a time of blossom in the plum, apricot and peach orchards, with red pheasants pecking among the bean flowers; a time of mud as the seasonal rains splashed high on the skinny shanks of the peasants planting out the rice shoots and the flanks of the blindfold buffaloes turning the water wheels. So a regular series of sploshes and creaks sounded from the fields, with dove and cuckoo notes (just like Surrey) and the thump of the woodman's axe from the hills, and everywhere the hisses and groans of overburdened men. For it was trading time too and along each slippery narrow path coolies humped their loads of up to eight catties (107 lb) which they were condemned to carry up to forty miles a day. Their cargoes were varied: straw, indigo, cotton seed, salt, sow-thistle, vermicelli, saffron, baskets of ducklings. The fluffy birds had been born on shallow trays inside huge earthenware incubating jars insulated by wickerwork and heated by a charcoal fire at the base. Up to four hundred ducklings at a time were hatched from each jar – after which warm arrival they were fattened on dried grasshoppers and sent to market.

Yangchow, which the Taylors eventually reached on 1st June, was a long-established trading centre; Marco Polo had once been its governor and had written in glowing terms of its active commercial and cultural life. But to the missionaries it was a 'rich, proud and exclusive city, and it contained a population of 360,000 souls still without any witness for Christ'. That June, every soul, Christian or heathen, was hot. Flies blackened the beggars' sores, the fishguts strewn along the canal banks and the pink sweetmeats stuck on the street-stalls. The Mission children got measles and lay itching and sweating in the bare, airless upstairs room of a back-street house they had eventually been allowed to rent. Then Hudson himself fell ill, and the baby daughter whom Maria took to Shanghai for smallpox vaccination got measles too, and whooping cough, and nearly died. 'My own Treasure,' Maria wrote to her husband from Shanghai on 10th July, 'is it that our tender Father is endeavouring to teach us by His present dealings lessons which He *might* take sterner methods to impress?'

Sterner lessons were to follow. By the time Maria returned to Yangchow at the end of the month, its citizens, who had at first been merely curious about the weird foreign intruders, were becoming hostile. Menacing town-toughs hung around outside the Mission door, bricks and mud were thrown at the windows and then yard-long yellow handbills were posted in parts of the city. These bills attributed a medley of startling misdeeds to foreigners in general and, in particular, to the newly-arrived 'brigands of Jesus'. The missionaries, it was announced, scooped out the eyes and livers of the dying which they mixed with lead and mercury to make silver, they opened orphanages in order to have a ready supply of young children whose vital organs were also used for this purpose and whose tender bodies the foreigners then either boiled to eat straight away or salted down for the winter in large barrels. The 'foreign devils' cut the foetuses out of pregnant women and from them concocted magical pills that would brighten the eyes of converts but act as a deadly poison to unbelievers.

This unsavoury mix of vicious calumny and superstition was typical of several that had already been disseminated at various times about missionaries, mainly, until now, about Catholics who had infiltrated in greater numbers further inland and had established a number of institutions such as orphanages. Such xenophobic eruptions were due to a complex combination of historical, political and social factors which became more prominent following the intrusion of more foreigners into hitherto inviolate parts of the country. The Chinese government, the provincial officials and literati, generally conservative by temperament, saw the intrusion as a dangerous threat to their security and prerogatives as supporters of the Manchu dynasty and as custodians of Confucian culture. Westerners, with their alarmingly effective technology, their outlandish ideas on law, religion and custom were bound to upset the status quo, and none were more likely to do this than the missionaries. In the first place, they were suspected of being secret political and commercial agents of the West; in the second, they certainly preached new and dangerous theories about the rule of one God and the responsibility of the individual soul. Both these concepts threatened those in authority. The first seemed to cast doubt on the semi-divine nature of the Chinese Emperor, the fountainhead of the dynastic power; the second seemed to propose a form of personal self-realisation and responsibility that could not but subvert the ordered, inflexible impersonalities of the Chinese social structure.

It was thus the local officials and literati who composed those particular bilious handbills which appeared that summer in the overcrowded streets of Yangchow. At about the same time, Will Rudland and his wife (one of the formerly 'unattached young ladies') arrived at the Mission, bringing with them, for all to see, a printing press and no less than four boatloads of household goods – to the stirring of mob hatred and fear was thus added the promise of loot. The tension rose with the temperature. Taylor's party, supplemented now by the Rudlands, George Duncan returned from Nanking's Drum Tower, and a newcomer, Gilbert Reid, stayed quietly indoors, having sealed all but one entrance to their rambling house. 'For the last few days we have been almost in a state of siege,' Emily Blatchley wrote. 'May God forgive these poor blind people and defeat Satan by making these disturbances the means of more widely diffusing the Truth among them.'

On Saturday 22nd August a rumour raged through the city that the missionaries had bought up twenty-four babies – to use, obviously, for their own nefarious purposes. Late that afternoon a mob converged on the Mission, quietly at first – shuffle of a thousand straw sandals, hiss of indecipherable whispers – then, as darkness fell, flame-torches flared to reveal dense swarms of anonymous faces, black eyes glittering, dark holes of mouths from which burst the first crazed howls of hatred: 'Child Eaters', 'Kill them', 'Foreign devils', 'Burn them'.

Taylor had already sent messages to the city yamen begging for guards to be sent, but none came and now he felt the only hope was to plead with the magistrate in person. He and Duncan managed to scramble down the back verandah and fly in search of aid, leaving Rudland and Reid to hold the front entrance. The two wives, both pregnant, Emily, the children and their native helpers cowered together in a candle-lit upper room. Missiles thumped on the walls, shutters splintered, plaster thudded and the roar of people hysterical with rage for blood and plunder chilled them to the bone. The women paled and trembled but remained calmly in prayer, supported by their conviction that it was no mere mob of Chinese toughs outside but the Devil's own legions manipulated by the powers of Darkness and Chaos. That being the case, their God of Light and Order would, eventually, protect them.

For a time it seemed unlikely. First Rudland came pounding up, his clothes torn and mud-splattered, shouting that the rioters had broken into the courtyard. Minutes later Reid called up, 'Mrs

Taylor, they are setting the house on fire and I can't help you.'
Maria grabbed their bedclothes, knotted them with shaky fingers,
then Rudland climbed to the verandah roof and lowered his heavily
pregnant wife and the children towards a hope of safety. Before
the rest could follow there was a thundering crash and the fore-
most rioters burst into the upper room. Maria faced them with
angry courage, demanding how they could bear to harm helpless
women and children. One of the men snatched Emily's purse from
her waist and Maria's wedding ring from her finger. The room
was full of smoke and men kicking open boxes, rummaging
through trunks. Outside on the roof Rudland struggled with a
man who clouted him over the head with a brick as he tried to
reach Maria and Emily. In the courtyard below, Reid tried to beat
back the people and the rising flames, shouting upwards, 'Quick,
jump and I'll catch you.'

The rope of bedclothes had been torn away and batteries of
stones met the women as Rudland helped them on to the verandah
roof, from which there was a jump of about twelve feet to the
yard below. Maria jumped, Reid half caught her and she fell side-
ways; Emily jumped and just as she did so a rock hit Reid full in
the eye. He staggered back concussed and Emily fell on her back
on the stones. Rudland, jumping down safely, helped the two
women up and managed to get them into a neighbour's house,
where the others were sheltering. Maria was bleeding copiously
and feared a miscarriage; Emily had a lacerated arm ('It is only by
God's great loving kindness that I have not a broken spine or
skull,' she wrote afterwards.); Reid, half conscious, seemed totally
blind in one eye.

Meanwhile Taylor and Duncan had long since reached the
yamen – rushing into the entrance hall crying 'Kiuming,
Kiuming!' [save life!], as the gatekeepers tried to barricade it
against them and their pursuers. For two hours, while howling
hundreds milled outside, Taylor argued with the magistrate,
answering with just-restrained fury such questions as what,
exactly, had the missionaries done with those twenty-four missing
babies? At length Taylor and Duncan were returned to the Mission with an armed escort, after being told that the rest of the

party had been massacred. 'When we reached the house the scene was such as baffled description,' Taylor wrote. 'Here a pile of half-burned reeds showed where one of the attempts to fire the premises had been made; there, the debris of a broken-down wall; and strewn about everywhere were the remains of boxes and furniture, scattered papers and letters, broken work-boxes, writing desks, dressing cases and surgical instrument cases, smouldering remains of valuable books – but no trace of inhabitants within.' A smell, ominously like that of burned human flesh, sickened the air.

It was not. Taylor found his companions still hiding in the next-door house, bruised, bleeding but unburned. That night they slept in the half-wrecked Mission and the next afternoon, still under escort, they gathered together their remaining possessions and prepared to leave. Maria wrote: 'As we passed out of the city in chairs Miss Blatchley heard some of the people say derisively, "Come again, come again." Yes, I thought, God will bring us back again, little as you expect it.' And that was their resolve: having once escaped the worst effects of the Devil's fury, they were determined to be tested again. So they went only as far as Chingkiang, the nearest treaty port, and there they obstinately remained, awaiting the first opportunity to return to hostile Yangchow.

But the view of the principal participants in the affair was a minority one. To most foreigners, especially British officials, the crux of it was that a group of Her Majesty's subjects living peaceably in a Chinese city had been physically attacked and their property destroyed, and that this attack had been more serious and brutal than any other made before then upon non-combatant Protestants in China. It was a flagrant violation of the rights granted to missionaries in the 1860 treaty and was clearly a case for the Consul. Soon it became a case for the diplomats in Peking and later one for the House of Lords and the columns of the London *Times*. This escalation of publicity resulted in a considerable distancing – by time and place – of the original action and its participants from the later ramifications and their participants. And the process, still common enough in any newsworthy dispute, had a familiar result: the original front-liners, the CIM missionaries, lost almost total control of the way in which the final outcome was handled and interpreted.

Mr W. H. Medhurst, Consul of Shanghai, started the snowball rolling by sending formal protests to the provincial officials in the area concerned. Not that Medhurst had any special love for missionaries, particularly for those who wore Chinese dress, which, he wrote, '... is calculated to lower the individual in the opinion of the natives and where it is employed also by female missionaries the effect is even more mischievous'. (The last barb refers to the fact that, in some parts of China, only prostitutes and Manchu women had unbound feet; foreign women in Chinese dress had unbound feet and were manifestly not Manchu.) And this all went to show, Medhurst continued irritably, that missionaries were not men of the world and their 'minds were apt to be warped by the engrossing character of their pursuits'. In other words, they were a bunch of wild-eyed, bothersome eccentrics – but they were British subjects and had a legal right to pursue their vocation unmolested which Medhurst was determined to see enforced.

So, when his early protests were ignored, Medhurst steamed off to Yangchow aboard the gunboat *Rinaldo* to investigate the scene of the riot and demand compensation for its victims and punishment for its chief instigators. Receiving no satisfaction, Medhurst went on to Nanking, where his negotiations with the Viceroy again broke down. By now it was a matter of national prestige; the Shanghai press was hot on the trail; Sir Rutherford Alcock, British Minister in Peking, ordered a flotilla of gunboats to sail up the Yangtze and show the Nanking officials who held the whip's handle. The CIM party watched all this huffing and puffing up and down river with some misgivings. They feared that they would become associated in the Chinese mind with the brute force of the gunboat upon which they hesitated to rely; they hoped that this was, perhaps, God's method 'of opening up the country to us for the spread of the Master's Kingdom', as Maria put it. And Emily, vacillating between vainglory and dismay, exclaimed, 'To think that all this unfurling of the Union Jack and gunboats etc. is about *us*!'

42

However, one of the questions raised by the Yangchow riot was whether it had been caused by them personally as a group of missionaries, or simply because they were the first group of Westerners to go and live openly in the city. Naturally, the missionary community preferred to believe the latter and the CIM received considerable sympathy from professional colleagues who pointed out that Taylor's party had not even begun to proselytise before the riot occurred – and obviously therefore the hostility was purely xenophobic.

But the missionary argument was partly irrelevant. The fact was that their presence in the inland cities *did* result in an intensification of anti-foreign feeling which would not have occurred if they had not been there. Sir Rutherford Alcock, seeing this clearly, pointed it up in one of his intelligent, long-winded definitions of the secular position. Alcock was a devout Christian, incidentally, married to a clergyman's widow, but his many years' experience in China and Japan had left him with a fairly low opinion of the 'spiritual capacities' of the Oriental and a sneaky suspicion that Christianity was not the only solution for the social and psychological ills of the East.

So his argument was that the handbills posted in Yangchow were plainly directed against missionaries in particular and that they had been instigated by the literati who rightly felt they had most cause to hate those who disseminated a disturbing new doctrine among the people. The missionaries were there, he wrote in a Foreign Office dispatch, and 'their doctrine is revolutionary . . . So why are they surprised if the ruling classes and literati oppose it with any means they can?' In Alcock's view the opening of the country to foreign trade was causing enough social upheaval and headaches for the foreign diplomats, yet missionaries wanted full liberty to evangelise and blithely assumed that 'all the liability and cost of their activity should be the government's . . .' 'If we accept responsibility for them then why should we not exert control over them?' was one of his many angry rhetorical questions. And, again, why on earth had the negotiators of 1860 ever allowed clauses about the toleration of Christianity to be so 'foolishly grafted on to a straightforward commercial treaty?' Christian

43

doctrine seethed with 'seditious implications' for China; nevertheless, he concluded angrily, 'it cannot be left to the irresponsible
missionaries whose sole duty is to God, to decide, irrespective of
international or material interests, whether China should have a
revolution or not'.

Alcock's opinion on missionary enterprise did not preclude him
from using the Yangchow affair as a test case that forced the
Chinese to accept the British citizen's right to pursue his vocation
outside the treaty ports. When, in mid-October, the Viceroy of
Nanking saw the guns of Her Majesty's Ships *Rinaldo, Icarus,
Rodney* and *Zebra* pointing at his city from the waters of the
Yangtze he re-opened negotiations and a settlement was eventually reached. The magistrate of Yangchow, who had long delayed
sending help to the missionaries, was dismissed and his replacement
issued a proclamation ordering the people to quietly accept the
residence of foreigners in their midst. It concluded: 'Anyone who
disturbs the public mind will be arrested at once. Be serious! Obey
with trembling!' Monetary compensation was paid to the CIM
group for their loss of lodgings and material possessions – including a concertina, a chignon and an ornament valued at £25, over
which items the Shanghai press made great play. As a final stern
reminder, a stone tablet was placed before the Yangchow Mission
(which the authorities repaired) stating that any 'irregular
entrance upon or interference with these premises will meet with
condign punishment'.

So on 18th November the missionaries returned as they had
vowed to – Hudson and Maria, Emily and the children and a
newly-arrived married couple – as vulnerable a little group as
before. Ten days later Maria gave birth to her fourth son in the
same house from which she had been forced to jump for her own
life, and his, three months before. 'God has given me the desire of
my heart,' she wrote. 'For I felt I would rather it were born in this
city, in this house, in this very room than in any other place . . .'
A legion of accusations can be levelled against the pioneering
missionaries, but even their sternest critics can hardly deny them
the quality of courage.

About the time that the CIM members recommenced work in

Yangchow and found their first 'candidates for baptism' among the neighbours who had given them shelter from the rioters, the full repercussions of the affair sounded in England. A long, rather biased account of it appeared in *The Times* and gave rise to a heated correspondence about the justifiability of military support for missionary activity in China. Obloquy was heaped on Taylor's party for their intrusive, reckless behaviour and their subsequent summoning of the gunboats when things got out of hand. They had been, and continued to be, intrusive and reckless, but it was not they who whistled up the gunboats, as Maria, writing to a friend at home, made clear. 'As to the harsh judgements of the world or the more painful misunderstandings of our Christian brethren, I feel the best plan is to go on with our work and leave God to vindicate our cause . . . The fact is that Mr Medhurst and through him Sir Rutherford Alcock took up the matter *without application to us*. The new Ministry at home censures those out here for the policy which the late Ministry enjoined upon them. It would be ungenerous and ungrateful were we to render their position still more difficult by throwing all the onus, as it were, on them.'

The change of ministry to which Maria refers was from the aggressive Tories to the Liberals whose general approach to Far Eastern affairs was less bellicose. Accordingly the new Foreign Secretary, the Earl of Clarendon, harshly criticised Medhurst and Alcock for their 'high-handed dealings' at Yangchow, and this led to an airing of the matter in the House of Lords and another heated row. The Duke of Somerset (whose speech was quoted with shocked outrage in missionary circles for years afterwards) said that he had '. . . a decided objection to this system of supporting missionaries in the interior of China. I object to it because it is unfair to the Chinese and I object to it because it places the commanders of our naval forces in a most unfavourable position . . . My noble Friends now in office wish to reduce the navy in China. Now if you reduce your navy you must reduce your missionaries, for almost every missionary requires a gunboat.'

Somerset went on to urge the recall of all British missionaries from the country because they were taking up the navy's precious time and prejudicing the interests of Her Majesty's trade. In any case, he concluded, 'a missionary must be an enthusiast; if he is not an enthusiast he is probably a rogue. No man would go and live up one of those rivers unless he were an enthusiast, and being an enthusiast he is the more dangerous.' The Duke compounded his sins in missionary eyes by blaming members of the London Missionary Society for the Yangchow fracas. This mistake he later corrected, allowing that the London-based mission was 'a respectable society' compared to which the CIM people were 'the very backwoodsmen of Chinese evangelisation'.

On the whole the Earl of Clarendon felt that the Duke was going a trifle far, but he agreed that the British gunboats were in Chinese waters 'to protect the floating commerce of British subjects against piratical attack' rather than to quench riots provoked by over-zealous evangelists, who, it seemed, 'often require to be protected against themselves'. He advised missionaries that they would do well 'to follow in the wake of trade when the people have learned to see in it material advantages to themselves rather than seeking to lead the way in opening new locations'.

The lordly clerics shook with fury at these accusations and, when able to get a word in edgeways, the Bishop of Peterborough angrily demanded of the Duke of Somerset if 'he, as a member of a Christian Legislature, would maintain that by becoming a missionary a man lost the rights of British citizenship which he would retain if he became a trader?' Surely all Her Majesty's subjects had the same rights under the treaty and were 'equally entitled to protection whether they sold cotton goods or bibles'? Wheeling on the Foreign Secretary, the Bishop demanded to know if the Minister would dare to suggest that missionaries follow 'in the wake of the *opium* trade'? And, in a final all-round salvo, he proclaimed that if, in the past, missionaries had always been 'prevented from becoming troublesome' then neither the noble Duke nor the other honourable members of the House, nor even he, the Bishop of Peterborough himself, 'would have been Christian at the present day'. No one came up with a convincing retort to this.

In its report of the debate the following day, *The Times* made its sympathies plain and its *de haut en bas* tone must have been gall in the throats of evangelistic status-seekers like Lewis Nicol. 'Missionaries,' the writer declared, 'are people who are always provoking the men of the world. We occasionally meet them at home and find them commonplace persons, not very well educated, not quite gentlemen, very much given to telling long stories the gist of which is that some native of somewhere once said, "Oh sir, how happy I feel! How I am indebted to you and Mrs Brown!" Graphic anecdotes of ex-cannibals who know by heart more texts than the most experienced Sunday school teacher form an interesting part of their annual reports and while these duly extract the guineas of their habitual patrons, they are apt to be received with unbelief and contempt by those who give the tone to political discussions. Parliament is not fond of missionaries, nor is the press, nor is general society. Some recent occurrences in China have tended to revive prejudice against them . . .'

The polished jibes of *The Times* still read well; the local press in China, attempting similar sophistication, succeeded only in being cumbrously rude about Taylor whose 'clerico-surgical character' was wasted on the Chinese and would be of far greater value in some charitable institution back home. 'Amongst the institutions of this kind which present themselves to our memory . . .' continues the Shanghai reporter, nudging his readers into full awareness of the approaching witty nugget, '. . . one stands out with exceptional clearness – the Hospital for Incurable Idiots. We wish Mr Taylor could obtain admission in some capacity to this excellent asylum . . . Were he an inmate, much trouble that now occurs would be prevented . . .' – in particular, of course, those mob riots which the treaty port residents blamed entirely on missionary intrusions. Nevertheless, as Taylor bitterly pointed out, 'when any of these outbreaks occur merchants and the foreign community generally partake largely of the benefits resulting from a clearer definition of treaty rights, while *all* the odium of having stirred up hostile feelings is thrown upon the missionaries'.

So the reverberations from that hot wild August night in Yangchow provided a sample portfolio of all the issues, misjudgments, sneers, theories, alliances and imponderables that were to reappear again and again following the long series of mob disturbances provoked by the presence of missionaries in the Chinese interior during the next thirty years. And, again and again, the same figures reappeared in due order on the troubled landscape: the provincial officials and literati revamping the same basic set of scurrilous propaganda, the town toughs muttering and gathering round mission doors, the mud-and-blood-spattered missionary flying to the yamen, the white-lipped wife feverishly praying, the frail, frightened children huddling in corners, the choleric consul summoning the gunboat, the local reporter wielding his jokey pen, the Chief in Peking exuding ponderous dispatches, the men at their Foreign Office desks in Whitehall eventually reading them. So each disturbance began and ended among the cool mandarins who instigated, hesitated, judged and misjudged until, about thirty years later, the whole scenario exploded in a welter of chaos and brutality, tears and blood, compared to which the Yangchow riot was merely a light-hearted prelude.

Few of the original participants were still around to make the comparison however, for thirty years was more than most missionary spans in China in those days. One of the first to succumb was Maria Taylor, thirty-three years old, long tubercular and almost constantly pregnant because of Hudson's passionate adoration of her. She died in the torrid heat of the following Yangchow summer after her eighth confinement. Cholera, womb haemorrhage, consumption of the bowels, she suffered them all with Hudson at her side to swab and succour and moisten the drying lips with brandy. When her last dawn showed Hudson the death on her face, he asked her, '"My darling, are you conscious that you are dying?" She was surprised. "Dying. Do you think so? What makes you think so?" "I can see it, darling." "What is making me die?" "Your strength is giving way." "Can it be so. I feel no pain, only weariness." "Yes, you are going Home. You will soon be with Jesus" . . . "I am so sorry," she said, and paused as if half correcting herself for the feeling. "You are not sorry to go to be with Jesus." "Oh no, it is not that. You know, darling, that for ten years there has not been a cloud between me and my Saviour . . . but it does grieve me to leave you alone at such a time. Yet He will be with you and meet all your need . . ."'

Again the set piece, the courageous and confident death handed on to the faithful like a talisman, cleansed of its stink and pain. It was not fashioned thus with conscious cunning, but grew naturally from the Taylors' mutual obsession with their divine mission. They felt themselves to be among the chosen, the blessed larger-than-life few. They wrung every last drop of meaning and savour from their mad endeavour and lived a full-blooded, high-pitched drama that kept at bay the perilous, barren meaninglessness of 'heathendom'.

Taylor underwent a confused spiritual crisis during the year of Maria's death and his writing of the time is threaded with the imagery of the dry soul thirsting for the river of God. 'Whosoever drinketh of the water that I shall give him shall never thirst' was the text that most sustained him and round which he embroidered patterns of comfort. After Maria's death he wrote, 'Twenty times a day perhaps, as I felt the heart-thirst coming back, I cried to Him, "Lord you promised! You promised that I should never thirst." And whether I called by day or night, how quickly He always came and satisfied my sorrowing heart.' He too fell dangerously ill and wrote of it, 'Yesterday in the cold stage of the ague, I was shaking until the bed shook under me; but I enjoyed such a vivid realisation that I was altogether the Lord's, purchased not with silver and gold – that I had not a particle of property, so to speak, in myself – that it filled my heart to overflowing. I felt if He wanted me to shake I could shake *for* Him; if to burn with fever I could welcome it for His sake.' The spiritual intensity of the medieval mystic burns through much of Taylor's writing – in his private diaries, his persuasive pamphlets, even everyday letters about money and recruits – and it was an essential element of his charisma that awed and attracted his followers. It sustained him through this crisis as it did many others in his life and within a few months of Maria's death he was able to write that he had made his peaceful pact with it, had found the secret of 'soul rest'. 'She is not lost. She does not love me less now nor do I love her less or less rejoice in her. And I do from day to day and every day so delight in the love of Jesus, satisfy my thirsty heart when most desolate from His fullness, feed and rest in green pastures in the recognition that His will has been done . . .'

The next year, 1872, just six years after the *Lammermuir*'s sailing, Taylor returned to England in search of more funds and members for the rapidly expanding Mission. He travelled home on the same steamer as Jennie Faulding, the adaptable, strong, sunny 'Miss Happiness' who had remained in Hangchow throughout to teach 'her boys' the elements of Christian doctrine and the words of her favourite hymn, 'There is a Happy Land'. Her pupils wanted to learn lots more English, she told her parents, and their favourite game was to sit astride a plank on rollers pretending they were 'riding in a foreign steamship'. But too thorough an acquaintance with the sophisticated and secular snares of the English language would, Jennie felt, 'expose them to great temptations in after life'. So she stuck to hymns and bible reading and encouraged a return to the traditional native games.

Her own ride home on furlough in a foreign steamship certainly opened new horizons and perhaps temptations, for, during it, 'Mr Taylor found the regard he had long felt for her develop into something more than friendship', as his biographers carefully put it. So by the time Jennie and Hudson got to London they were engaged, and tongues must have wagged in the heads of some who remembered Moule's accusations about those goodnight kisses in Hangchow.

Tense, quiet Emily Blatchley, the other recipient of those tokens of affection, wrote in her journal soon after the engagement was announced, 'I feel sure from what I know of my own nature that I should, if I had had the chance, have been Mrs . . . And so it is in love and mercy my God cut off my flowing stream at which He perhaps saw I should drink too deeply. Such a sweet sweet stream, such a painful weaning! Therefore such a great blessing must await me for Jesus to bear to see me have so much pain.' Bereft and tormented, she was reduced to one burning final need: to prove the bounty of the 'great blessing' which was to be her reward. And that, at least, was not long denied her, for, left in London to look after Hudson's children when he returned to

China with his new wife, she died of tuberculosis within a year. 'A true heroine . . . an instance of noble Christ-like self-sacrifice for the good of others. Her memory is fragrant . . .' was the tribute paid to her in *The Christian*. But she, who burrowed deeply into herself, would not have sanctioned this. 'Men suppose me, call me, good, self-denying, happy, trustful and *satisfied*. Oh Christ, was ever child of Thine more vile and miserable!' was among the last entries in her scrappy passionate journal.

The deaths of Maria and Emily marked the end of the true frontier days for the China Inland Mission. By 1874 the surviving loyal members of the *Lammermuir* party were the old hands who showed the ropes to the grand total of its hundred new workers. The total included missionary wives and Chinese helpers but not the seventy mission children whose bellies had to be regularly filled. And so Taylor, like all leaders of growing organisations, found himself increasingly swamped with the administration of money and manpower; it was the price he paid for his undisputed authority and success.

But CIM 'successes' – like those of every other Protestant and Catholic society in China – were, to the soul-thirsty evangelists, a few pin-prick-size oases in a vast desert of disinterest and dislike. Those missionaries who, in moments of honesty or despair, paused to consider the full implications of their position, might have dismally recalled the judicious words of Sir Rutherford Alcock who nailed a commonsensical lid on all their ambitions: 'I cannot without a total disregard of history,' wrote Sir Rutherford, 'hope that missionaries will accomplish more with the Chinese in this nineteenth century than has been effected with far more ample means and under far more favourable conditions in the West during the preceding eighteen. What 30,000 pulpits and preachers cannot do in Great Britain at the present day is not likely, as far as human means are concerned, to be accomplished by two hundred or three hundred teachers of an alien race and of different and conflicting sects, however earnest and devoted they may be.'

'Human means . . .' That was the little qualifying crack through which all missionary hopes brightly gleamed. For they were counting on *super*human means, on portents and miracles and

PART TWO

And it all seems to have meaning, even the broken
*   machinery,*
The abandoned oil wells, the rowboat sunk in the ice
*   of winter . . .*
Is this waste, this debris, a necessary part of our energy?

The Notebooks of Theodore Roethke STRAW FOR
THE FIRE

CHAPTER FIVE

Upon the Plain of Chihli

Sir Rutherford Alcock left his post in Peking at the end of 1869, about the time that the fat Foreign Office file on the Yangchow Riot was stored away in its appropriate cabinet. As a final salvo, Alcock reported a remark made to him before his departure by Prince Kung of the Imperial Court – a remark which provided such a convenient and pithy introduction to the whole subject of Western intrusion into China that it was quoted many times by later writers. For the benefit of those who have not yet heard it: 'Take away,' said Prince Kung to Sir Rutherford, 'your missionaries and your opium and you will be welcome.'

Kung had little to gain from the disruptive forces of foreign trade or religion because he was a member of the ruling Manchu dynasty, a brother of the former Emperor Hsien Feng. It was the sickly Feng who, until his death in 1861, had for favourite concubine that fabulous, rapacious, beautiful, brave and wily woman Yehonala (The Orchid). By 1869, as a result of some masterly and ruthless intrigue, Yehonala was co-Regent to her infant son, the Emperor Tung Chih, virtual ruler of the Empire and adorned with the title of Tzu Hsi, the Motherly and Auspicious Empress Dowager. She was later to be known as Old Buddha, in ironical recognition of her sagacious staying power and was eventually to be called various unprintable names by foreigners who suffered from the dire effects of her intermittent xenophobia.

Kung, however, was no xenophobe, rather an astute and realistic statesman who understood that China had to come to some sort of peaceful, workable terms with the West. In 1861 he created the Tsungli Yamen, the first ever Chinese Foreign Office which had the sweeping sub-title of 'Generally-managing all-countries business-matters praetorium'. It was none too soon to establish some such institution because, following the 1860 treaties, representatives of all the major Western powers came to reside in Peking and they needed an office with which to communicate – even though, in Westerners' view, the Tsungli Yamen staff were expert in the art of elusive and non-committal non-communication.

To those wide-eyed diplomats from London, Washington, Paris, St Petersburg, the Chinese capital must have seemed a wild and wondrous place indeed. It was walled against the plains and was divided into the Chinese or Outer City and the Tartar or Inner City by other walls that were broad enough for foreigners to use for that most un-oriental habit of the daily constitutional. Inside the Chinese city the indigenous inhabitants rubbed grubby shoulders with Koreans, Russians, Manchurians, Nepalese, Tibetans and Mongolians. Impenetrably and doubly enclosed inside the Tartar City shone the looping yellow-porcelain roofs of the Imperial palaces, wherein lived the formidable Empress Dowager with her huge entourage of councillors, handmaidens, courtiers and eunuchs adept in the arts of dissimulation, spying and poisoning.

Mongolian camels were a feature in the city, with their great spongy feet, two huge humps apiece and a chubby Tartar rider wedged between. The animals' long tresses swayed as they moved and in summer, when they became unappealingly patchy, soft balls of shed hair fluttered and rolled about the dusty streets like little brown animals. Acrid dust, the colour of camel's hair, was another feature; foreigners all grumbled about it. During the hot season it blew in thickly from the surrounding plains, blotted out the sun, whipped down the wide main streets and through every split in the paper-glazed house windows, through every tiny crack of the closed green sedan chairs where minor mandarins quietly curled, and every wrinkle in the hides of the imperial elephants (sent each year as tribute to the Emperor from the King of Siam) was clogged with it.

Then in July the rains rolled up from the Gulf of Pechili, the elephants merrily trumpeted and moist lizards flicked over the courtyards of Confucian, Buddhist and Taoist temples. Soon there was too much rain: the wattle shacks of the poor tended to literally dissolve in it; standing pools of side-street sewage overflowed and harnessed animals sometimes floundered to their death in them. Snow came and the River Peiho, main line of communication with the coast, froze; longed-for letters from the outside world were sent by wagon from Shanghai and took thirty days to reach the foreign legations. The execution grounds outside the city walls were slippery with the sodden remains of the recently disembowelled, and the surrounding plain was a pitted quagmire through which the springless mule litters thumped and sickeningly rolled.

Aboard a tottery two-mule litter one day in the autumn of 1863 the Reverend Joseph and Mrs Edkins of the London Missionary Society reached the capital, and became the first Protestant missionaries to establish permanent residence there. When describing missionary 'firsts' the qualification 'Protestant' is usually advisable; in the case of Peking it is essential because Roman Catholic missionaries had maintained some kind of outpost there almost continuously since 1601. In that year the redoubtable Matteo Ricci had arrived and founded the first Jesuit mission; soon after, his colleague, Verbiest, constructed the famous astronomical observatory on a terrace against the city wall. Its globes, zodiacs and quadrants still remained in the 1860s, their rusted and neglected condition a reminder to the Protestants of how far ahead of them the Catholics had been and, also, of how little the earlier offerings from the West had been prized. The Catholics were still much in evidence, their headquarters around the large cathedral Pei-tang. The cathedral was to be sacked in the holocaust at the end of the century and, until then, contained the unique natural history collection assembled by the Abbé David, a priest who rode off on donkeyback to Mongolia each summer in search of ornithological rarities such as half-ruffed lilac doves and frizzled pelicans, and is still remembered for Père David's Deer, and *Davidia involucrata*, the handkerchief tree.

With this background of Catholic influence, it was hardly surprising that Joseph Edkins found it difficult at first to explain to the people the difference between his version of Christianity and the Catholic. He had however the advantage of being a Sinologue for he had been in the country since 1848; he had travelled as far north as the Yellow River, visited the Taiping leaders with a young Welsh colleague, Griffith John, and published a book on *The Religious Condition of the Chinese*. This work, which first appeared in 1859, was in widespread use as a textbook up until the end of the century, but it was certainly not an impartial one, as its sub-title suggests: 'With Observations on the Prospects of Christian Conversion among that People'. As a translator, Edkins soon became embroiled in the 'term question' about what was the most appropriate Chinese word to use for 'God'. The Jesuits had first used a name that meant 'Lord of Heaven'; the English Protestants, determined to define a difference, selected 'Supreme Ruler'; the American Presbyterians, last on the field but equally individualistic, settled for 'The True Spirit'. Missionaries engaged in much learned controversy over such issues – 'logolatry' was the laymen's definition of it – but on only two points could all Protestants agree: first that the Catholic word was certainly wrong, secondly that the existing situation caused needless speculation in the Chinese mind about how many Christian gods there really were.

In order to spread the word about his own Congregational Protestant God, Edkins bought a Buddhist temple beside a grain market. It was a dilapidated building in a large courtyard with a still-fearsome bronze dragon snarling from each roof corner. The resident priests were turned out and Edkins saw to it that they took all their 'idols' with them; then he hired labourers to build lots of dividing walls and generally renovate and whitewash. He confessed to some surprise that the Buddhists had so readily agreed to the Christianisation of their temple, and the smell of incense must have long lingered among its rafters. But no roof dragon snapped, no dispossessed ghostly bonze disturbed his slumbers –

perhaps because, as he explained in a letter home, 'Buddhists have no sense of exclusiveness as we do'.

Edkins opened the front hall as a street chapel with benches set on the broken stone floor and a simple pulpit from which he preached daily. A great curiosity he was at first, and all the rice-sellers and sellers of millet and its stalks, buckwheat, beans yellow and dried, conjurers, thieves, strolling musicians popped in for a peep when business was slack, and others – snot-nosed urchins, beggars, smelly old women, scabby-skinned outcasts – who had no business, came and stayed for as long as the show lasted. Edkin's young wife started a little school for girls to whom she taught the rudiments of Christian doctrine, a smattering of geography and English. Unlike Jennie Faulding, Mrs Edkins felt that English was a valuable acquisition for her pupils, and thus the two women reflected on a small scale the great division in the missionary mind about the teaching of English to the Chinese at all levels.

The one faction saw English as a mind-opener for the Chinese which would encourage them to assimilate Western moral and spiritual values; it would be niggardly and indeed cowardly to withhold it on the grounds that it brought secular temptations in its train. In any case, as one speaker at an early missionary conference put it, 'Is it not dishonest to use education as a mere cats-paw to induce pupils to come, while the sole object is not to educate them but to Christianise them?' Fundamentalists like the China Inland Missionaries however, whose avowed sole object *was* to Christianise without Western trappings, maintained that English did but exalt the intellect, not the spirit, and that it served to separate the few who learned it from the masses of their own kind.

Allied to this question was the equally vexed one regarding the teaching of the Chinese classics. The classics were the very warp and woof of the nation's cultural life and yet much of what they contained was, in the missionary view, false and idolatrous. 'We cannot get along with the Chinese classics and we cannot get along without them,' as one missionary succinctly put it. A compromise often resulted whereby students at missions were taught the classics in traditional fashion by a Chinese teacher during the week and, every so often on Sundays, the missionaries preached on the theme of how much falsehood and superstition the venerated books contained.

A favourite school primer for English instruction was *Peep of Day*, first published in 1870. It contained 'Early Religious Instruction', for the 'Infant Mind' of the West and so, hopefully, was suitable for the older but 'raw heathen mind' of the Chinese also. Its message was somewhat stark: 'At last Jesus will sit upon the white throne and everyone will stand around His throne. He will open some books in which He has written down all the naughty things people have done. God has seen all the naughty things you have done. He can see in the dark as well as in the light and knows all your naughty thoughts. He will read everything out of His books before the angels that stand around. Yet God will forgive some people because Christ died upon the Cross. Whom will He forgive? Those who love Jesus with all their hearts . . .' But what about Mother and Father? Was that what the slant alarmed eyes of the children mutely asked as they listened? Certainly a few pondered deeply upon such matters and among such few the missionaries moulded their most zealous converts – and their bitterest enemies.

Considering the kind of instruction, it was hardly surprising that even converts were often reluctant to send their children to the mission schools, and this was particularly the case with girls who, when they married, would be completely absorbed into their husbands' families. To educate a girl was like sowing the field of some other man, like putting a gold chain round someone else's puppy, as the sayings went. So, until the end of the century, mission schools were about the only places where girls could obtain any kind of formal education. To attract them, missionaries often offered free needlework classes during which, as one lady missionary put it, 'our Bible women have constant access to our heathen pupils'. This, she continued, gave an opportunity to 'subdue with loving firmness their restless garrulity, halt their frivolous questions and bring them to a more passive condition' – one more favourable to the process of sewing and sowing.

But this and other free instruction offered to both boys and girls were seldom sufficient inducements and until the 1880s it was fairly common practice to actually pay the 'heathen' pupils to attend school, a method justified by its advocates with the slogan 'if there were no paying there would be no praying'. The missionary hope was that once the young heathen mind had been convinced of the superior qualities of Christianity, the child would go willingly to school, without payment. But this strategy often proved a built-in disincentive to the very end the missionaries sought, for, in the event, the attendance-by-payment system made it more difficult to separate the truth-seeking, God-fearing sheep from those capricious and money-grubbing goats who, once they had been paid to learn sufficient English at the mission school, went skipping off to some lucrative job as a clerk in a foreign hong or consulate and never opened their Bibles again.

Among adults too, missionaries found it hard to distinguish between true converts and Christians in it for the perks, and some sort of instruction and examination in the elements of doctrine were usually required before full church membership was granted to 'enquirers'. However, as the missionaries were under constant pressure from their home-based societies to produce ever longer lists of converts, and as any such list might typically include folk like an itinerant seller of water-chestnuts, a peasant grandmother, a wig-maker, a laundry maid and the youngest son of the chapel gatekeeper, the level of attainment had to be fairly low and the interstices of salvation's net fairly flexible. In any case, as one missionary speaker reminded her colleagues, it was the indwelling spirit, not the unpromising external envelope which was important: 'The women in your care may be old, blind, bound-footed, degraded, stupid, yet if God has stamped them as His, then take what He has given you and make the best of it!' In this situation, missionaries tended to be somewhat reticent about the standards of understanding they required from aspiring Christians, but one, William Soothill, a Baptist, did publish a few examples of the sort of questions he put to them: 'Whom do you worship now?' 'How many gods are there?' 'Where was Jesus born?' 'How many disciples are there?'

This vexed question of quantity versus quality was an early cause for dissension among missionaries in China. Some felt that it was only by reducing the complexities of their creed to a few simple messages that they could hope to attract numbers of converts; others feared that this approach would only increase the antagonism of the educated classes who assumed they were being fobbed off with superficial fairy tales. At the day-to-day level of missionary work similar differences of opinion arose – between, for instance, the Reverend Joseph Edkins of the LMS and his colleague in Peking, Doctor John Dudgeon. Dudgeon, as his name suggests, was an emotional and touchy man of very strong opinions and he was soon telling his Home Committee in London that some of the church members were very dubious characters and that Edkins 'had no fortitude to dispense with the opium smokers, rascals and other hangers-on' whom the Mission had attracted. One 'convert' decamped with all the school furniture one night, and another 'goes along with his tail up, down at heel and no jacket, prying into Mrs Edkins' bedroom and circulating stories about her relationship with her own cook!' Edkins, Dudgeon concluded tartly, was inclined 'to forget that many followed Christ for the loaves and the fishes'.

Another very relevant factor, which neither mentioned directly, was undoubtedly that the small hospital and dispensary which Dudgeon opened soon proved far more popular and successful than Edkins' preaching chapel, and if Edkins had dispensed with all his 'hangers-on' the numerical gap between 'his' converts and Dudgeon's might have been much greater. Even so, the Mission's records for the year 1868–9 were not too impressive: baptised in the year (children and adults), 34; unpaid preachers, 6; catechists, 2; students, 3; schoolgirls (day and boarder), 17; dispensary assistants, 3; church members under suspension, 4; disappeared during the last five years, 33.

Faced with such figures, the missionaries had to put the blame somewhere and had it always been on their own heads they could scarcely have sustained the continual weight of failure. No shadow of reproach could be attributed to their omnipotent and infallible Master, so they blamed each other, or the obdurate imperviousness of the Chinese, or the men who issued directives from secure wood-panelled committee rooms in St James's or Salisbury Squares.

Edkins was unhappy with the situation because he felt, perhaps with justification, that the China missionaries were the poor relations of the LMS. Glamorous and wondrous deeds were being performed in Africa in the wake of the Society's most famous missionary, Dr Livingstone; shoals of converts were being safely landed in the Pacific Islands; mission schools and hospitals were multiplying in India. 'But in China you seem to require that each of our little outstations show the vigour of manhood while yet in infancy . . . without supplying us with the needful funds for their proper maintenance,' he complained. Furthermore, while on the subject of funds, how could the Directors expect his paltry allowance to meet all the Peking Mission's burgeoning expenses – a wage for the married catechist, travel expenses for colporteurs, printers' bills, school furniture, chapel helpers' fees, salary for the Chinese pundit, servants' wages, rent and dispensary items, not to mention food for everyone and the cost of long-overdue renovation of their private living quarters? 'Our floors in the dining and sitting rooms are still unlaid after three years of occupation . . . We are worse situated in this regard than any other missionaries in China. Deal kindly with us for once!' Edkins pleaded, furious, as most missionaries were, with the tight control that the home directors exercised over the purse strings.

Jonathan Lees, Edkins' colleague in Tientsin, shared these views as he made quite clear during a long correspondence about a fuel allowance for his chapel. The Home Committee ruling was: 'Native Christian communities should supply what is necessary for warming chapels where they meet for worship'. To which Lees, in a fine old rage, exclaimed that his house cost £35 per annum to heat and how could they expect 'some twenty or so peasants keeping families on about 8d a week' to keep the chapel heated as well? He continued, 'We are hedged in by minute and vexatious regulations which turn us into mere machines for whom lofty motives – honour, truth, gratitude and love – are as nothing compared with the danger of breaking some pettifogging rule or over-spending by some trifling amount.' It may have been this outburst which provoked a secretarial comment to Joseph Edkins that 'Some of our brethren seem to think that money maketh success . . .'

The difficulties and misunderstandings of this nature which most missionaries had at some stage with their societies at home were partially due to the overall system of organisation which modern sociologists would classify as 'centre-periphery'. All decisions regarding the movement of personnel, allocation of funds, adoption of new methods were taken by the home committees and, as mails were slow and committee-meetings infrequent, up to nine months could elapse between the submission of a request and the response to it. It was intensely frustrating for the active evangelist hopping about on the periphery wanting to go ahead with a particular project – which he sometimes did, anyway. Then a row often resulted, for, as has been pointed out, what looks like enterprising creativity at the periphery may, from the centre, look suspiciously like insubordination. (One reason for the CIM's success undoubtedly was that Hudson Taylor never fully adopted this system; in the early days he embodied all authority in himself and moved about with it; later he put his administrative offices in Shanghai, not London.)

But to Jonathan Lees of the LMS, waiting for decisions on various matters from a head office that was going through a particularly dilatory phase, everything seemed to be deteriorating. Throughout 1869 he felt an increasing chill of antagonism among all Tientsin inhabitants. The local authorities refused to let him rent a building for a dispensary; merchants in the foreign settlement spurned his plea for donations so harshly that, he decided, '. . . no heathenism is so hard to reach as theirs'; as for the Mission itself, 'our hearers are few and timid, enquirers are rarely met with and in our own church a baptism the Sunday before last was the first for nearly twelve months'.

Seeking the hope of untilled fields, of which China had a plentiful supply, Lees made a preaching tour in the spring across the plain of Chihli. The flat lines of its stretching landscapes were broken only by glittering pyramids of salt from the marshes, by junk-sails twisting along the River Peiho and by the thousands of grave-mounds humped everywhere. Later, Lees wrote a poem about his numerous travels in the area which certainly makes it sound pretty dismal; but he was an inveterate, versatile grumbler and a good accumulation of discomforts and difficulties always brought out the literary best in him.

> Let those who vote Lake Como 'slow'
> Or grumble on the banks of Po
> And wonder where they next can go,
> Try the great plain of Chihli.
>
> But it were best to leave behind
> All hopes of an aesthetic kind;
> Eye, ear or nose small joy will find
> Upon the plain of Chihli.
>
> And as to equipage – alack,
> No Pullman's car on even track
> Or easy chaise with cushioned back
> Has yet been seen in Chihli.
>
> A two-wheeled cage, four feet by three
> Holds man and traps; for he
> Sits on them *à la turk*, you see
> That is the mode in Chihli.
>
> The carriage lacks both door and springs
> Upon its shaft Wong sits and sings
> To cheer his mules – tall bony things
> Reared on the plain of Chihli.
>
> The leader swings his tail with grace,
> Now kicks, now breaks his hempen trace,
> Four miles an hour his constant pace
> Upon the road in Chihli.
>
> Enthroned within the cart, you try
> To look o'er Wong's broad back, and spy
> Perhaps three feet of clear blue sky
> Which, after all's not Chihli.

Creeping outside to mend your view,
You find earth wears her earthiest hue,
And that ere long you're earthy too
Like all beside in Chihli. . . .

It does go on; about the inn-meals of ox-hide swimming in oil or bony fish caught in a pit; about the whisker-freezing north-easters or the sloughs of mud; about the summer nights on brick-hard inn-beds 'where rats and other game abound, Indigenous to Chihli'.

The indigenous humans, not beset with wistful yearnings for Pullman cars or dinners of roast beef, were, during Lees' spring tour, thoroughly enjoying themselves at the rice-planting festivals, and the rhythmic thump of drum and squeal of bamboo pipe vibrated in the pale sunshine. Everyone was dancing and some of the peasants were, Lees wrote, 'in a kind of frenzy, their whole body in motion'. Stilt-walkers wearing painted masks tilted and swayed above the jollifications; wine-happy men staggered round carrying platforms decorated with bells and orange tassels on which squatted dusty clay idols; the central attraction was often a man dressed in gaudy women's clothes, stuffed in a wheelbarrow and being mockingly courted by the local yokels. To Lees, such spectacles were a sinister, spine-chilling reminder of the hysterical, lewd, pagan element in Chinese life which the missionaries most loathed and feared. And they did so with reason, for the same spirit that fanned the painted faces and bawdy antics of the villagers also infused, at a more sophisticated and malevolent level, the anti-Christian propaganda which, that same spring, again began to appear in some parts of the country.

Most of the tracts emanated this time from proud, self-contained Hunan, the most xenophobic of all the Chinese provinces, and noted for the breeding of the most aggressive and courageous soldiers. The tracts were in the national tradition of anti-heterodox propaganda in that they accused Christians of fermenting political and social unrest, and practising various sexual aberrations. There was some pretty strong stuff in them by any standards, so strong

66

7   A group of bible women

8   Opium smokers

9 & 10 The Cambridge Seven: (*from left to right*) *standing*, C. T. Studd (1), Montagu Beauchamp (7), Stanley Smith (4); *seated*, Arthur Polhill-Turner (6), Dixon Hoste (2), Cecil Polhill-Turner (5), William Cassels (3) (the numbers refer to Fig 10)

11 Heywood Horsburgh, in travelling dress

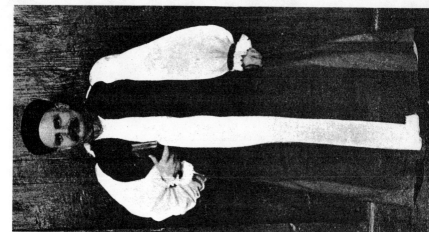

12 William Cassels, Bishop of Western China

13 James Gilmour equipped for Mongolia, in February 1884

14 Howard Taylor and his wife, Geraldine Guinness

15 A Chinese woman's foot in its binder and shoe compared with an English woman's shoe

that for many years no full English translation was published, and perhaps this was as well, if one considers what effect it would have had on, say, a young lady missionary recently emerged from the shelter of a Devonshire rectory.

The best-known tract originally written about 1861, was called *Pihsieh chi-shih*, that is a record of facts to ward off heterodoxy and translated by missionaries as 'The Death Blow to Corrupt Doctrines'. It attributed to missionaries just about every obscene practice that a race with very long experience of men and manners could dream up, and cunningly combined with them modicums of truth and fragments of common hearsay. Roman Catholic priests were all sodomists and, to take their pleasures more conveniently, they inserted tubes into the anuses of young boys to enlarge them; 'they take out the tube at night however, which they call "preserving the constitution"'. The Protestant clergy, most of whom were manifestly heterosexual, exercised a sort of *droit de pasteur* over every young bride in the church, giving her 'a holy introduction to the net of pleasure'.

To increase enjoyment of such practices, missionaries brewed special concoctions made from male seminal fluid, women's menses and crushed ovaries cut from young virgins. These magic potions were also rubbed on the genitalia of women converts and made them so sexy that they flung themselves on the missionaries, who were adept in the 'art of prolonging orgasm which they call seeking to become genii'. The male missionaries apparently needed to seek greater strength because their generally chivalrous manners towards 'the fair sex' suggested to the Chinese the fanciful notion that foreign women were highly esteemed and overruled their menfolk. This, the tract continued, was partly because menstrual blood was considered a precious gift, 'and the barbarians vie with each other to drink it – which accounts for their unbearable stench'; they also smeared their faces with it before worshipping the cross. Converts were initiated into the Church with 'a private washing by the pastor with holy water, which occasion he used to gratify his vile lusts'. Then the initiates were given four ounces of silver and a pill which 'confused and darkened the mind' so that they destroyed their ancestral tablets and worshipped instead 'the image of the naked child who points one finger towards heaven and the other to earth'.

The writer of the tract, who called himself 'the most sorrowful man on earth', then went on to argue forcefully against somewhat garbled extracts from Christian teachings, and to ask some quite awkward questions, such as, if Christ's mission was to save the souls of the world, why did he wait until the second year of the Emperor Ai Ti of the Han dynasty before being born? In conclusion the writer provided a full catalogue of 'Christian vices', with cautionary tales of the dire fates that awaited all who came in contact with them. For example, 'In Li-chow recently there was a rebel who had the power to make himself invisible and who, by means of black magic, cut off the queues of men, the nipples of women and the testicles of little boys . . . Were you to ask the victims about this they would in some cases say, "I saw a priest wearing a cross on his chest. When he struck me I fell to the ground and immediately becoming dizzy could not stop him from doing what he did." All the women and boys who were injured thus suffered terribly upon reviving and often died before the day passed.'

This clever, sinister, offensive tract was widely circulated among provincial officials, school teachers, headmen, in the coastal areas and Peking and exacerbated the latent hostility against Christians – especially against Roman Catholics. This was because the Catholic influence was, at this time, still more pervasive and insistent; also the French government supported its missionaries with an uncompromising vigour unmatched by the other Western powers, which they did partly to counter-balance the greater trading and economic power of Great Britain. It was the French who, during the 1860 treaty negotiations with the Chinese, had pushed missionary rights furthest to include the important concession that their Catholics be permitted to rent and purchase land in all the provinces and erect what buildings they wished. The concession appeared only in the Chinese version of the treaty however and applied to missionaries of other Western countries only because of the customary 'most favoured nation clause' (which it is doubtful that the Chinese understood). Thus the actual right of British and

American missionaries to purchase land and build in the interior was somewhat tenuous – not that this stopped most of them from taking advantage of it and demanding consular protection if they were opposed.

However, in 1870 only a few backwoodsmen like the CIM members were seeking to establish their 'rights' in the interior, and most Christian endeavour was centred within the treaty ports. At Tientsin, for example, there were two mission compounds of American Presbyterians, the Reverend Jonathan Lees and his colleagues, and a strong contingent of Catholics. The Sisters of Saint Vincent and Saint Paul maintained an orphanage, and several priests lived near the imposing church of Notre Dame des Victoires which stood on the site of a razed Buddhist temple. Early that summer, soon after Lees returned from his trying itinerations, the city boiled into a cauldron of anti-foreign rumour and conspiracy; several children in the orphanage died in an epidemic and a number of kidnappings were reported which, it was said, had been instigated by missionaries. The hoary tales about their gross appetites for children proliferated; foreigners were insulted in the streets and their homes attacked.

On 21st June the French Consul stormed off to the yamen to protest to the magistrate and, in the ensuing rumpus, stupidly fired a pistol at a minor official. An uncontrolled mob gathered outside and, on leaving the yamen, the Consul and his assistant were stabbed to pieces. Banging gongs, screaming, brandishing sticks and swords, the people then charged on the French Consulate, the church and the orphanage – looting and firing the buildings and killing every French person in sight. Two priests were murdered and ten nuns were raped, had their eyes gouged out and their breasts cut off, before being chopped up and thrown into their flaming orphanage. The Protestant chapels were looted and fired and that night Jonathan Lees sat up on his veranda with a loaded pistol at the ready. The next day gunboats came blustering into Tientsin harbour and, for a fortnight, Lees wrote, 'threats of further violence were heard on every hand'. The atmosphere remained jittery for the rest of that precarious summer and there were other xenophobic outbreaks, but none to equal the violence of what became known as the Tientsin Massacre, which brought France and China to the brink of war.

They might have teetered over it, but, that same summer, the French found themselves at war with the Prussians, and thus with little thought to spare for the dismemberment of a few nuns on the other side of the world. So stiff indemnities were imposed instead and eighteen Chinamen, supposedly the ringleaders of the massacre, were beheaded at the Tientsin execution ground. The authorities, Lees complained, allowed relatives to sew their heads back on their bodies so that they would appear unmutilated in the next world. 'They should have been ignominiously displayed in pieces,' he added angrily, 'and instead there is even talk of erecting a temple in their honour!'

Had such a memorial been raised to the murderers of the Catholic missionaries, it would probably have attracted many subscribers, for the majority of the people, from the Imperial Court downwards, simply wanted all missionaries out of the way. The Empress Dowager, speaking from behind the traditional yellow silk curtain to the Viceroy who was coping with the aftermath of the Tientsin affair, remarked, 'It would be a fine thing if we could secure ourselves properly against invasion. The missionary complications are perpetually creating trouble for us.' Hints like that, from such an august source, were not disregarded, and, the next year, the Tsungli Yamen issued a circular to all the foreign powers about the whole question of missionary activity in China.

The document laid most of the blame for the repeated disturbances on the Catholics, alleging that they refused to let their converts 'abide by the laws and customs of the country'. It went on to point out that the common people couldn't distinguish Catholics from Protestants or indeed from other foreigners, so that all were endangered whenever missionary-incited trouble brewed. To ease the situation the Tsungli Yamen ministers suggested that all Catholic orphanages should be closed, that missionaries should conform to native institutions and come under the control of local officials, that converts should be treated like all other citizens for tax and legal purposes, that Chinese women should be for-bidden to enter foreign churches, that all the female missionaries should be sent home.

The proposals were drastic but they showed that the Chinese were seriously trying to dig out the roots of the missionary problem. It was true that orphanages aroused distrust and hostility, true that some missionaries, particularly Catholics, interfered in defence of their converts, lawsuits relating to the payment of taxes levied for 'heathen festivals', true that the presence of native women in churches and the comparative freedom of women missionaries to travel and teach offended Chinese standards of propriety and lent support to the tales of Christians' lewd and indecent behaviour.

But for the Western powers to accept the proposals would have implied their retreat from a position of strength, which they saw no valid reason for doing. So, after a number of compromises had been offered and rejected by both sides, the Chinese, who lacked the military or political power to enforce their demands, had to drop them and the 'missionary question' went back into the simmer of 'masterly inactivity' that was to last another thirty years. As Paul Cohen, a modern historian, put it, the tortuous, emotional, ineffectual debate that followed the massacre '. . . revealed in clearest terms the profound gulf still existing between Chinese and Western concepts of law, religion, liberty, society and man. When viewed in this perspective it would appear just as myopic to brand the Chinese proposals as a tissue of lies as to charge the foreign missionaries with callous indifference to Chinese sensibilities. Each side operated on premises they had believed to be universally valid and both were caught up in a clash of cultures over which neither had much control.'

CHAPTER SIX

A Man for Mongolia

A month before the Tientsin Massacre, when the dry heat quivered tensely over the comfortless Chihli plain, musk melons grew gold and sweat dripped down the skinny frames of the coolies as they lifted, gathered, swept and carried, a new recruit arrived at the LMS mission in Peking. His name was James Gilmour, a rangy, twenty-seven-year-old Scot with a vigorous constitution, a quirkish ense of humour, a blunt manner, a conviction that alcohol was the Devil's own potion and a burning belief that his task on earth was to spread the Gospel Word among half a million or so Mongolians. He came swinging into the Mission compound radiating self-confidence and a fine disdain for the petty squabbles over funds and methods which often went on there. 'Let it be understood at once,' he wrote in his first letter to the Home Committee, 'that for money I don't care a single straw, my one idea is being a missionary and I only need enough to keep me in reasonable health.' How the Committee must have loved him for that, after the stream of complaints they usually received about financial stringency, and how Edkins and Lees must have shuddered at Gilmour's high-minded naïvety, and how, eventually, Gilmour probably regretted that letter as he bitterly began to learn that zeal alone, however burning, was not enough.

But in the beginning it seemed to be, and after barely two months in the capital, Gilmour went charging off in a mule cart towards Mongolia, announcing that the 'unsettled state of Peking' following the Tientsin Massacre 'rendered his onward journey imperative'. The truth was that the man had an absolute obsession with the Mongolians, even though they were, according to Wells Williams, the first Protestant missionary to describe them, '. . . a stout, squat, swarthy, ill-favoured race of men, with short broad noses, long teeth distant from each other, thick short necks and nervous muscular thighs . . .' In other ways too they were infrangible material for conversion, being quite uninterested in any new ideas whatsoever and assenting placidly to the religious authority of the lamas, whose form of Tibetan Buddhism held the entire country in thrall. But: 'the Bible tells us to preach the Gospel to every creature – and that must surely include the Mongols?' Gilmour asked some time later after his enthusiasm had been repeatedly crushed by the hard shell of Mongolian indifference and his tone was becoming shrill and uncertain.

'To every creature . . .' was the biblical injunction quoted more often than any other by missionaries, and there were always a few originals like Gilmour who yearned to find and nurture their very own tribe of 'creature', to whom they could give themselves unreservedly, for whom they could be the first, pristine St Paul. So 'Gilmour of Mongolia' – as he soon became known in mission circles, though not in Mongolian – went to live near Kiachta and after months of silence informed the outside world that his only needs were a supply of Mongolian Bibles and an 'outpouring of the Spirit' upon the poor people.

The land Gilmour had chosen for the proving of his Christian mettle was among the harshest in the world, predominantly brown, yellow and white, dotted with sheep, camels, horses, oxen and the occasional felt tent moored in the middle of nowhere and enclosing a few Mongols huddled round a fire of animal-dung. Gilmour was offered board and lodging in one such tent by a lama who had no sense of religious exclusiveness, and there began to learn the language through intimate, abrasive contact with the everyday squalor of Mongolian life.

It began at frigid dawn with the hiss of re-kindled fire and the smart of eyes opening on a pall of wood-smoke from the previous night's embers that still hung below the vent in the tent's top. Then a clump as the iron pot filled with snow was dumped over the new day's flames; the snow, Gilmour mentions, had been gathered just outside the tent and thus 'contained all manner of impurities, and sometimes, at the bottom of the pot are found things which anybody but a Mongol would consider very objectionable'. A handful of brick tea was thrown into the water to boil and then the lama's servant poured it into a pail, brushed the pot's side with an aged horse's tail, melted some mutton fat in the same pot, added a quantity of brown meal, then poured the tea in again to re-heat. Breakfast was ready: a porridgy mush of brown 'meal-tea' which was the Mongolians' sole fare until sunset – except, Gilmour says, on the last day of each year, when they made up for it by eating seven dinners in twenty-four hours.

Men encased in sheepskins with ear-muffs clamped round their dirt-and-wind-cracked faces tramped in and out all day – to look at the weird foreigner, eat some tea, enjoy the usual Mongolian chat. It centred on the ferocity of their dogs, the health of their herds or the size of their debts, for most of them spent what little money they ever got on fermented mare's milk and cheap Chinese liquor. 'My chief here won't lend me nine shillings to buy a sheep-skin coat for my old woman – so I reckon she'll freeze to death this winter. My (blank) chief won't lend me anything . . .' is Gilmour's bowdlerised translation of a typical Mongolian grumble. He listened, noted down everything, but left a lot of blanks in his English renderings for, he explained, the Mongols used 'a vast amount of impure language which is simply the expression of corrupt thought'. But corruption was the Devil's own work and thus not invincible; so he continued his language learning, longing for the day when he could blanch the dirty Mongol tongue with the pure milk of the Gospel word.

At sunset, when the rheumaticky herdsmen brought the calves into the tent to keep warm and the immemorial silhouette of a camel caravan was etched against the dusky sky, the servant went to the dog-proof cage outside wherein were hung frozen carcasses of beef and mutton. Lumps of meat were hacked off, boiled in the all-purpose pot, plonked on a board and eaten with a knife. While Gilmour and the lama industriously chewed, the servant added millet to the water in which the meat had boiled for a second course of millet-gruel, and, 'I have seldom before or since tasted any preparation of civilised cookery that proved so delicious,' Gilmour concluded. Back in Peking, he used to ask his friends to a supper *à la mongolian* at which this gruel was the *chef d'oeuvre*. Unfortunately he couldn't persuade them to share his enthusiasm and the story went that one missionary, knowing what was coming, refused to say a pre-prandial grace on the grounds that it would have been quite dishonest to express his gratitude to the Lord for it. But the Mongols slurped their gruel with delight, then belched, peed, and rolled their greasy grubby bodies into sheepskins beside the whimpering calves and dogs. As the last act of the day, the servant threw a jarful of charcoal on the fire which 'burned splendidly and everyone used to lie and look at it with a glow of satisfaction and gradually drop off to sleep'.

For the next two years James Gilmour spent much time in Mongolia, riding from one encampment to another through the pleasurable, tedious procession of nights and days, 'Sunrise and sunset have their glories much like those seen at sea; stars and moon have such charm on the lonely plain. Ever and anon you come upon tents, discoverable at night by the bark of dogs – in the daytime seen gleaming from afar and indistinct through the glowing mirage. As you sweep around the base of a hill you come upon a herd of startled deer and give chase to show their powers of running; then a temple with its red walls and ornamental roofs looms up and glides past. Hillsides here and there are patched with sheep; in the plains below, mounted Mongolians are dashing through a large drove of horses pursuing those they wish to catch with a noosed pole that looks like a fishing rod. On some lovely stretch of road you come upon an encampment of two or three hundred ox-carts, the oxen grazing and the drivers mending the wooden wheels, or you meet a long train of tea-laden, silent camels.'

He became inured to a state of perpetual cold, damp, dirt, and adapted his tough frame to the roll of camel, spring of horse, bump of cart; he learned to recognise the wolf's yowl from the hills, the goatsucker's cry, the wail of the female camel at twilight, what the men shouted as they tethered, bridled, fed their herds; he even stopped worrying about the lumps that lurked in the bottom of the cooking pots – but he couldn't accustom himself to the Mongolians' total disinterest in his message. In late 1873 he wrote home, 'In the way of direct results there are absolutely none . . . I can say I have not yet seen a single Mongol anxious about his soul. I have seen hundreds working out their own salvation as they suppose – prayers, offerings, pilgrimages – but no one at all concerned that Christ should save him . . . The reflex influence of this is that I have got "the Blues" and that badly.' It was autumn again when he wrote that, a hopeless time in a hopeless place. The pastures were seared and whitening in the wintry winds, bearded vultures with yellowish abdomens hung in the grey skies, a few horsemen, purpled with cold and wadded in skins, moved about the horizons – stolid men who didn't want to know about Christ.

Gilmour went back to Peking to break his 'blues'. He decided that to convert the Mongols he must travel yet further and more vigorously and distribute Western medicaments – which were the only gifts they welcomed from him. So he needed money after all, for the hire of carts, camels, guides and for medical supplies. 'It is little short of nonsense for one solitary man to announce the opening of a Mongolian Mission as you suggest,' he told the Home Committee, who undoubtedly thought how enterprising it would look in the Annual Report. 'Wherever I put it the people would wander off once their animals had eaten the pasture round about . . . So should I go or stay?' he demanded, in large capitals, to know. 'I'll leave you to answer and meanwhile I'll go on.'

Meanwhile, too, Gilmour decided to try something else to cheer him up: a wife. These were the days before missionary conferences and interdenominational group holidays in the hills provided fruitful hunting grounds for bachelors and widowers in search of eligible god-fearing young ladies, so Gilmour turned for help to his friend, the Reverend Meech, another young member of the Peking mission. Meech must have been as mild as his name, for he did not get involved in the continuing fratricidal controversies there, but got landed with the administrative chores instead; more immediately to Gilmour's purpose, he already had a wife, formerly Miss Ann Prankard.

Adorning Mrs Meech's harmonium were pictures of Mrs Prankard and sister Emily who ran a little school for gentlewomen at their home, Devonshire Villa, Bexley Heath, Kent. Gilmour, a frequent visitor to the Meeches' drawing-room, used to gaze wistfully at Emily's picture and beg for extracts from her letters. Soon, with his customary directness, he decided he wanted to marry her, though they had not even corresponded. So he wrote to ask. 'If she cannot come there is no great harm done,' he told his parents. But Emily Prankard left Bexley Heath like a shot and came, and was married to Gilmour in Tientsin the following summer. 'Without any gammon,' he wrote to a friend soon after the wedding, 'am much more happy than even in my daydreams I ventured to imagine.' For, luckily, his Emily was 'a jolly kind of body and she does not take offence'.

The boundaries of Emily's jolly resilience were to be reached the following spring when she accompanied her husband to Mongolia. This time he was equipped with three ox-carts (one having a straw awning 'for Mrs Gilmour's greater comfort'), two blue cloth tents, medicines and coloured pictures of biblical scenes – for experience had forced him to admit that 'the portions of St Matthew's Gospel of which the unassisted Mongol can make sense at all are comparatively few'. In fact, he usually found them trampled in the mud outside his tent next day. It was exciting at first to be 'fairly launched on the plains' where every living creature was an event: rock partridges cackling along the verges, a grey snake among some violet irises, ground squirrels kicking up the dust near their tunnels. It was a land speckled with the yellowish – antelopes and rats, faded lemon of lama's robe, amaryllis and daphne among the gulley stones, and sulphur butterflies over ochre alluvial mud; sheep's wool on the herdsman's back yellowed with age, and wind-dried bones of the dead whose flesh had been eaten by wolves, vultures, dogs or eagles. Occasionally they met a pedlar on donkey-back selling Chinese alcohol and obscene stereoscopic pictures printed in Shanghai, or a weather-beaten woman in high leather boots carrying pails of mare's milk, and quite often they met a lama travelling and preaching like themselves.

Gilmour allowed that the Buddhists taught a humane regard for life, a healthy understanding of the meaning of sin and a touching faith in immortality, but he deplored the corruption of the lama-filled temples that were, in his view, 'gilded cages for unclean birds' where sodomy and syphilis were rife. Lamas made up sixty per cent of the male population, he estimated, and thus 'the energy of the country is clogged and crushed by the incubus of just as many men as can manage to find standing-room on the super-stition and piety of the people'. Still Gilmour was fired by the 'hammer and tongs' of theological debate, and some of his happiest hours in Mongolia were spent huddled in some smoky tent arguing the relative merits of Christianity and Buddhism with one or two of the 'arrogant, bigoted and self-sufficient' lamas. Once a lama accused Gilmour of having a mind 'like the mouth of a flour-bag bound up and drawn together and so constricted that nothing can enter . . .' which Gilmour gleefully repeated to show his readers just how arrogant and narrow-minded these bonzes were.

Poor Emily found the nomadic life most trying. One of the tents had been intended for 'our retirement and Mrs Gilmour's personal use', Gilmour explains; but this seemed very stand-offish to the Mongols who had no acquaintance with the word privacy. So the Gilmours found they had to 'keep literal open house; at our meals, our devotions, our ablutions, there they were – very much amused and interested of course'. After they had been travelling about a month, the most demoniacal storm Gilmour ever experienced burst over them. Carts overturned and wheels spun, animals uprooted their tethers and whinnied away, tent-cloth ripped; they cringed under their sodden bedding for two days, dug channels between their weighted-down boxes to pre-vent them from being swept away in the howling torrents that seethed around them. It was all very different from dear old Bexley Heath and Emily, after bearing up gamely for two sum-mers, decided that she must leave the salvation of the Mongols to her husband.

This meant that she and their new-born son now needed larger, more permanent quarters inside the Peking Mission. As a result there blew up one of those inter-fraternal disputes which shamed and worried all those concerned at the time and, in retrospect, provides a fair illustration of the sort of difficulties and issues that arose as an increasing number of younger missionaries arrived to join the pioneers – bringing with them new ideas, expectations, demands. This particular battle was on two fronts: territorial and ideological.

By the mid 1870s, the LMS station in Peking had expanded from its humble beginnings to an unwieldy collection of buildings that housed the Meeches, the Gilmours, the Edkins and the Dudgeons who kept producing daughters. ('Did I mention the birth of a fourth daughter to Mrs Dudgeon last month and third for us this?' Edkins asks the Home Committee in a weary PS.) There was a hospital, a dispensary and a communal chapel, and each family had its own separate living quarters, plus guest-room, study, nursery, servants' rooms, private courtyard. But James Gilmour lacked a study, and when Dudgeon was away on vacation, he turfed the doctor's clobber out of what seemed a storeroom and installed in it his desk and his Mongol pundit who was helping him to translate hymns into Mongolian.

When Dudgeon returned to this state of affairs the extent of his ire was extraordinary. 'Gilmour has turned me out of my study and laboratory and medicine store and book depot and rest-room!' he stormed in explanation of the room's indispensability. 'He has dumped my drugs in an outhouse – the very apple of my eye and I consider them too sacred to be touched by other hands.' Upon which Gilmour, as obstinate and argumentative a man as Dudgeon, stuck his heels into his new study and refused to budge. The atmosphere at the Mission became ridiculously tense; the two men stopped speaking to each other and refused to attend the same committee meetings, which caused difficulties as the committee was only five strong at the best of times.

Then Mrs Edkins died of cancer. Like most of the other missionary wives she left no personal records of her endeavours, probably because she was too occupied with the organisation of her household, the girls' school, Bible and sewing classes for women and the production of female offspring. As she lay dying, her weeping pupils gathered on her veranda to sing 'Safe in the arms of Jesus' and 'There is a land that is fairer than Day'; when she died Edkins was stricken into months of silent withdrawal and everyone mourned her 'saintly and selfless devotion to duty'. She must indeed have been a source of calm commonsense and unity within the Mission for after her death its members split into irreconcilable camps: the Dudgeons and the sorrowing Edkins versus the sisterly-joined Gilmours and Meeches.

So total was the lack of communication that it was decided to call in an 'independent arbiter' and the choice fell on Chester Holcombe, Secretary of the American Legation. Holcombe solemnly inspected the whole property and produced a written report in response 'to the request made to me to express an opinion as to the right of occupancy of a certain *3-chien* room in the LMS'. The report stated that though Dudgeon had more work and more children, he had more room already and Gilmour should be allowed to keep his study. At this, Dudgeon, who in Meech's view was 'truly losing his mind over the matter', turned very nasty indeed. Why, he demanded, did Gilmour need such living space when he had but one child though 'he has been married four years and at the rate of past progress he cannot utilise all his available rooms for a dozen years to come . . .' Finally he announced that if Holcombe's verdict wasn't reversed he would 'sever his connection with the Society'. At this threat Gilmour flounced out of the disputed territory and plonked his desk back in the room he had wanted to reserve for 'Mongol guests'. He was, he told the Home Committee, 'surrendering the room, I hope as a Christian should, with a sweet temper, and yet *I feel sore on the whole subject*'.

But clearly Gilmour's Christian temper did not always prevail, for Dudgeon soon found that, though he had his study, he had no friends left. 'I am still in a painful position with my brethren,' Dudgeon complained after his pyrrhic victory and, in the hope of reinstating his position, he wrote a whole pamphlet on the subject and had it privately printed in Shanghai. This madness alienated even Edkins who was fearful that such 'sorry evidence of missionary strife' would leak to the local press and provide a field day for the junior reporters.

The pamphlet was divided into three parts: first, The Question of Dr Dudgeon's drug-room and study (in which all the Mission's accommodation and its use is described in detail); second, The Question of Consent (in which Dudgeon denies Gilmour's assertion that he ever gave his approval to the changeover of the room), third, the Question of Arbitration (in which Chester Holcombe gets a real drubbing for being such a 'thoroughly biased judge'). That they all had fairly spacious ideas of what was necessary for comfort is apparent from Dudgeon's suggestions of various alternative locations for Gilmour's study: the 'second lumber room' perhaps, or 'the old boys' school quarters near the cowstance', or let Gilmour move his cook and wife into the bathhouse and use half the large kitchen as a study, or 'let him pull down his woman's room and erect a two-storey building on it', or build 'on any piece of the east courtyard that doesn't overlook me'. He, Dudgeon, had nowhere for his catechists and medical students to stay, yet 'Mr Gilmour keeps insisting on a guest-room for Mongols and their camels. Now Mr Gilmour doesn't consider himself a Chinese missionary. Why then should our space be devoted to Mongols and their beasts of burden – of which we are never likely to see any?'

Dudgeon's pamphlet makes both sorry and hilarious reading at this distance – all that ballooning vindictiveness about the use of one small walled space in the vast city of Peking, a space which, to thousands of its inhabitants, would have seemed palatial home enough. Nor were those concerned unaware of what a spectacle they made and the guilt and shame of it added to their frustration. Gilmour deplores the fact that after '*three years* this unseemly squabble still goes on', and Meech, in one of his rare outbursts, tells the Home Committee that 'something is paralysing our work here . . . No baptism has taken place for a long time . . . I sometimes fear it is the judgement of God upon our divisions and disputes . . .' In 1880, Joseph Edkins, quite worn down with bitterness and melancholy, resigned from the Mission staff and became a translator for the Imperial Customs Service, a defeated return to the secular world for which many missionaries never forgave him.

That a dispute over the use of one room should have so many long-term consequences seems peculiarly silly, but real disagreements on matters of principle underlay its apparent triviality and deepened the dimensions of bitterness on both sides. They showed, for instance, in Dudgeon's sly crack about the Mongolian guests who never appeared, for, as the doctor eventually admitted, he had lost confidence in the whole concept of a Mongolian mission. Both he and Edkins were of the opinion that the most efficacious policy was to create fixed centres for evangelisation, education and the provision of medical aid which would attract the people to them – whereas Gilmour spent weeks riding about trying to find someone to preach at. And did not Gilmour's 'success rate' speak for itself? 'Fruit NONE; not even leaves' Gilmour confessed to the Home Committee after *six years* of effort. Basically, Dudgeon laid such obstinate claim to the disputed room because he was convinced that his medical work was a more valuable and effective tool for the task of Christianising China than anything Gilmour, the wandering evangelist, had done or was likely to do.

As the century progressed, the adoption of more broadly-based humanitarian methods of evangelism increased and missionaries learned to make use of the traditional Chinese association between benevolent institutions such as hospitals and the preaching of philanthropic and religious principles. But in these days medical missionaries were still much in a minority – there were only ten fully-qualified mission doctors in the country in 1874 – and they had to defend their work against the fundamentalists who affirmed that 'medicine should never be more than the handmaid of evangelism', that it was no substitute for 'the simple going forth and speaking of the Word'.

This of course was Gilmour's view, but when he took the 'handmaid' medicine to the Mongols, he found to his dismay that she made his evangelising almost superfluous. 'They [a Mongol tribe] had come so far to ask for my medical help and waited so long,' he confessed once, '. . . that I could hardly find it in my heart to make them wait still longer while I preached to them first . . . The truth of the matter is that they want the missionary only insofar as he is a doctor . . .' And that was a bitter pill for Gilmour, who had come to China with such a grand conviction that when the Message glowed from its messenger aright, it alone was strong and clear enough to attract and illuminate even the most apathetic and sin-encrusted Mongolian soul.

CHAPTER SEVEN

Where are the Nine?

Mr E. H. Parker was a consul with many years' experience in China and a great respect for the Chinese, whom he found to be 'quiet, industrious, patient, orderly people', who made some of the 'finest all-round citizens on earth'. Like most laymen who held such views, he had little time for missionaries who, he thought, should cease their vain endeavours to disrupt and discredit one of the world's richest and most ancient cultures and, instead, 'minister to drunken sailors and others of their own kind in the treaty ports who obviously require corrective discipline'; better yet, they could go back home and work among the 'thousands of lost ungodly souls that inhabit the slums of such cities as Manchester and Chicago'.

Parker was in Peking for a spell during the early 1870s, staying in the five-acre-large British Legation compound where visiting-cards circulated in relentless hierarchies among the staff bungalows and everyone was talking about the American wife of the French Minister who was reputed to have shot her first husband and whose loud perfume and outrageously immodest ball-gowns would, had she been in dear old Europe, have precluded her from being invited anywhere. Few visiting-cards passed between the legation and missionary compounds, and Parker undoubtedly reflects the diplomats' prevailing tone of sniffy, amused derogation when he sums up the Protestant missionaries in Peking as people who 'do good in the following ways: they teach poor children to be clean, speak the truth and behave themselves chastely; they translate various books into Chinese, they discourage vice and they are useful as interpreters to those legations who have no proper staff of their own . . .' However Parker, again like most critics of missionaries, made an exception for their medical work. He mentions that the LMS hospital in Peking was 'generally looked upon as an unmitigated influence for good', and he confesses a puzzled esteem for a man like Dr Dudgeon who several times refused offers to go into private practice in the foreign settlements where he could have earned four times as much money.

Dudgeon had opened his first hospital in 1865 along the wide, main Hataman Street, with, on one side, the Chinese Customs Office directed by the formidable Sir Robert Hart and, on the other, the Great Lamasery where more than a thousand lamas told their elephant-bone beads and foreign visitors were graciously offered the best part of the fatty sheep's tail hooked out of the noonday broth by the Chief Lama himself.

Like most of the early mission hospitals, Dudgeon's was overcrowded, under-ventilated and abominably noisy. There was an out-patient department where those waiting to see Dudgeon listened to Bible readings – about which a native helper questioned them when they got inside the consulting room. The walls of the wards were inscribed with Christian texts, including a few in illuminated paint especially 'for the comfort of those who couldn't sleep at night', and communal services of hymn-singing and prayers were frequently held. In addition, native evangelists or young missionaries visited each patient to read passages from the Bible and sometimes, as one described it, 'to ask them about the books that are lying about and urge them to pay attention to these things'. Woebegone Chinamen with dishevelled queues lay on the straw pallets and accepted such painless indoctrination without complaint, and sometimes with enthusiasm, for it was a small concession to make in return for the free Western-style medical treatment which they could not have obtained anywhere else.

The Chinese were disease-ridden, a condition which, in the eyes of some evangelists, was both result and punishment for the extent of the 'moral corruption' among them. Missionary doctors, however, gallantly coping with the frequent epidemics of typhoid, diphtheria, typhus and cholera, were more inclined to lay the blame on the filthy state of the urban areas where main thoroughfares were ' no more than elongated cess-pools', as one doctor put it. During epidemics, he added, the people organised 'gaudy idolatrous processions designed to propitiate the evil spirits supposed to cause disease, while the germs actually responsible bred in the gutters and streets through which they parade'.

Smallpox, the 'divine black flowers' scattered by the goddess of disease, was as common as measles, but much more dangerous. In North China every other face was punched with its scars and the unmarked girl went cheap on the marriage market because of the high risk that she would contract it later and then the husband would be put to the expense and trouble of a funeral. Skin diseases of a less fatal nature were also rife and the mission doctor dealt with pussing sores and fiery rashes every day. Eye cataracts and dyspepsia were other common complaints, the latter caused, in one doctor's opinion, 'by the velocity with which the Chinaman thinks food ought to be propelled into the stomach'. Rich men sidled into the consulting room asking for aphrodisiacs when a course of their own 'three genital pills' made from the ground-up penises of dogs, asses and deer (for hardness, strength and length) had not produced the desired result. Knotted, rotting lepers, for whom nothing could be done, propped themselves against the doorways, and such was the faith in the miracle of Western healing that the dead were sometimes brought too, in the last hope of revival. All corpses were discreetly and quickly disposed of and desperately ill patients were seldom admitted because the populace was prone to hold a hospital responsible for a death and, if several patients died in rapid succession, it could cause a xenophobic riot. Nevertheless the mission hospitals were usually full – if only because the calling in of a native doctor was invariably a more hazardous and painful undertaking.

The Chinese of the time didn't rely much upon a knowledge of anatomy and their ruling principle was to cure by a system of sympathetic compensation. Thus pieces of flesh were sometimes cut from the body of a healthy child to give to his dying parent, and the sinews of horses or tigers were administered to restore strength. Doctors came with a variety of peculiarly nasty tonics – real witches' cauldron concoctions that contained frogs' bellies, red-marble filings, calves' bladders, plum kernels, snakes' necks, rabbits' pellets, and were presumably designed to take the patient's mind off his other troubles. There were specialities: river otters for syphilis, bears' paws for coughs; blood from the head of a just decapitated criminal was soaked up into orange-size pith-balls and sold as 'blood bread' (a profitable side-line for executioners); any carpenter afflicted with ulcers would be cured by chewing a few bits of ancient cement from Canton's Flowery Pagoda. The people, rightly a little sceptical of all this, perhaps took wry comfort from their proverb that 'Medicine only cures the man who is fated not to die'.

Such primitive medicine horrified missionary doctors and most of them tried to start some form of student training in Western medical techniques. The training was naturally combined with Christian teaching and the proportions of the combination were a matter for anxiety and dispute. As professional men, they longed to disseminate far and wide the value of anaesthetics, antiseptics, anatomical study, but as evangelists they had constantly to ask themselves whether they were right to concentrate on the saving of bodies rather than souls. The majority usually did more healing than preaching because they were unable to resist the pressure of the suffering and misery around them. But many a time they reached the same bitter conclusion as Gilmour, for when their patients, who had seemed to swallow Christianity along with their medicine, walked out of hospital cured, very few were ever seen again in church or chapel.

Medical missionaries also tried to win the allegiance of the people through their efforts to cure opium addiction. Following the Opium Wars, the British continued to import large amounts of opium into China from India. Pure Patna or Benares opium had always been a luxury for the wealthy, but from the 1860s onwards increasing quantities of cheaper, homegrown opium came on the market so that its use was increasingly widespread – and respectable. Business men used it as a social lubricant during tricky transactions, as their Western counterparts resorted to whisky and soda; in addition, 'the attractive and ritualistic smoking paraphernalia itself imparts an air of leisured consequence', as Dudgeon shrewdly noted. Each city had a quantity of opium dens with names such as The Hall of Life's Renewal or The Spring of Everlasting Solace that conjured visions of oriental potentates on silken couches being wafted into some exotic dreamland, but, in fact, most of them were squalid shanties frequented by the poor. In their dim and smelly recesses seething pans of opium bubbled over charcoal fires and skinny coolies crouched on the mud floors rolling pea-size balls of the treacly-looking stuff into their pipe-bowls and sucking desperately, their eyes forlorn and glazed.

There was considerable disagreement among Westerners about how harmful opium was to the Chinese. Merchants and other interested parties took the line that it was much less ruinous than the gin that flowed in the back-lane grog shops of every Western industrial city. Missionaries however, particularly the medical ones, attested that the continual use of opium resulted in loss of muscular power, bowel troubles, asthma, impotence and a 'total collapse of moral values'. The difference of opinion was an extension of the position in Britain where there was a strong protest lobby, actively supported by all the major missionary societies, against the business interests that profited from the trade. A Society for the Education and Stirring Up of Public Opinion against our National Opium Trade was started in the 1850s and its letterheading bannered the slogan, 'The Proud Flag of Albion is marked with One Broad Black Stain'. Certainly the Chinese called opium 'foreign mud' and rightly blamed the British for introducing it to the country, though this did not prevent numbers of provincial officials from quietly making money by the growth and sale of some locally popular variety.

But many Chinese were ashamed of their addiction and came willingly to missions that offered hope of cure. In response to demand, Dr Dudgeon opened a side-street shop which sold anti-opium pills (together with Christian tracts and books on Western philosophy), but these pills invariably contained a quantity of morphine which was just as habit-forming and rather like 'changing one's tipple from colonial beer to methylated spirits' one critic suggested. Dudgeon's pills sold well however and he used the profits to open an opium refuge near his East Gate dispensary. The haggard 'opium sots' were confined in these refuges for up to three months at a stretch and were either cut off from the drug at once or it was doled out to them in diminishing doses. To ease the pains of withdrawal, which the addicts likened to the perpetual gnawing of wolves at the vitals, they were given Doctor Osgood's or Doctor Peck's quinine and belladonna pills, plus, in the words of a missionary write-up on the theme, 'ample opportunities for reading and innocent amusements such as stereoscopic pictures of New Testament stories and suitable music'. Most of the smokers who sought Dudgeon's help were middle-aged men and they said they had taken to the drug years before – as relief from pain or to help them forget their business debts or their disappointment at a lack of male offspring.

Women seldom came to the refuges, though some smoked opium and considerable numbers used it each year as an ultimate weapon in their hopeless struggles against social oppression. Chinese women had always been prone to suicide, a death that would, they believed, result in their becoming avenging spirits with powers to wreak vengeance upon the harsh mothers-in-law or husbands who had driven them to self-destruction. To die by opium overdose was, as Dr Dudgeon once wrote, 'quiet, painless and effective; it does not obtrude offensively upon family or neighbours, its soothing anodyne and soporific properties give no opportunities for a change of mind . . . and it is in every way better than the old clumsy methods of swallowing gold leaf, lucifer matches or mercury, throwing oneself in a well, taking lead to break the bowels, cutting the throat, stabbing the abdomen . . .' The average number of attempted opium suicides admitted to the LMS hospital each year was 150, but there were no national statistics to prove or disprove Dudgeon's contention that the number of such cases was increasing because death by opium was so comparatively easy.

Nor was any official correlation made between the prevalence of female suicide and the native custom of foot-binding, but there must surely have been one, because it was a custom that condemned growing girls to years of continual and sometimes excruciating pain. When the child was about six years old, a professional binder was called in to wind the first lot of wide bandages round her feet in such a way as to crush the toes back under the sole and make walking almost impossible. The bandages were removed once a month for washing, the deadened skin was sloughed off and at each binding the toes were driven further back towards the instep. It was pitiful to witness little girls who had been rosy-cheeked and active, grow pallid and listless from distress and lack of sleep as they sat helpless indoors all day, often clutching at the bandages and rocking to and fro with the pain caused by the hindering of normal growth. The whole process took about four years, during which the instep bones cracked and often broke. After it, the feet remained about three to four inches long and the woman would be a cripple for life, able only to hobble painfully on what looked like little dead white hoofs.

Naturally, missionaries detested this barbarous custom and were in the forefront of the movement for its abolition, but progress was slow because the whole weight of social custom was behind it. Oddly, the ruling Manchus did not adopt it, but nor did they actively suppress it, for they were aware that it encouraged the people's tendency towards submission and inertia. Indeed, Li Hung Chang, one of China's leading statesmen, once incautiously joked to a Mrs A. Little, President of the Anti-Footbinding League, '. . . you know if you unbind the women's feet you'll make them so strong and the men strong too that they'll overturn the dynasty!' So the women of the rulers walked big-footed and free, but among the Chinese the possession of the so-called 'golden lilies' was a mark of caste from which only the lowliest peasants and prostitutes were exempt. 'A large-footed woman,' it was explained in an etiquette guide written, of course, by a man, 'goes from house to house with noisy steps . . . she has to do rough work and does not sit in a sedan chair . . . when she goes out she is wet by the rain, tanned by the sun, blown upon by the wind and is without fame or honour.' These might seem fairly minor burdens compared to bound feet, but Chinese mothers wanted to display their eligible, attractive daughters 'like flowers, like willows, with their feet bound short so they walk beautifully with mincing steps, swaying gracefully, showing they are persons of respectability'. And thus, among the numbers of incurables that Dudgeon had to turn away from his hospital, few were more heart-rending to him than the young girls whose legs and feet had developed ulcerated gangrene or simply mortified and dropped off as a result of too-tight binding, and who would never walk again like flowers or like willows.

Dudgeon spent about thirty years in his Peking hospital. Every day he, and those of his colleagues engaged in similar work, stumbled among the bags of rice, the vegetables and teapots that each patient, however poor, insisted on bringing into the ward; they smelled, each day, the same effluvia of filthy bodies, dysentery, ulcerating sores; they heard, each day, the wails of the fever-stricken, the murmurings of Bible-reading evangelists, the hum of innumerable flies round the privies; each day they prayed that at least one of the hapless creatures to whom they ministered might genuinely and lastingly 'declare for Christ'.

Some did, but the numbers of converts did not rise in proportion to the increasing amount of effort expended. In 1876, the Protestant medical missionaries reported that 41,000 patients had been treated in their sixteen hospitals and dispensaries; by 1889 the figures were sixty-one hospitals, forty-four dispensaries and 348,439 patients. But only a very small percentage of that large last figure became converts and the most heartfelt hymn among medical missionaries working in China was, and remained for many a year, 'Where are the Nine?'. It refers to the story of Jesus healing the ten lepers, only one of whom sought salvation after being cured. Its first verse went thus:

> Wandering afar from the dwellings of men
> Hear the sad cry of the lepers – the ten,
> 'Jesus have mercy' brings healing divine;
> One came to worship, but where are the nine?
> Were there not ten cleansed? Where are the nine?

CHAPTER EIGHT

A Man of Sympathies so Broad

There are very few Protestant missionaries of the nineteenth century whose names still appear in modern histories of Sino-Western relations; one of the few is Timothy Richard. Son of a Welsh farmer who was an ardent Baptist, Richard attended a school built next to a Congregational Chapel in one of his father's fields till he was fourteen. Then, acting on his own initiative as he did throughout his life, he made a schoolmaster of himself, later talked his way into theological college and sailed for China as a Baptist missionary in 1869. Four months after his arrival, the only other remaining representative of the Baptist mission – that had been sorely decimated by disease – died of typhus; at his funeral service in Chefoo Richard heard the warning guns that fired to announce the news of the Tientsin Massacre. He was twenty-five years old, with a very little knowledge of Chinese, the only living Baptist missionary left in the country.

Nineteenth-century Baptists, with their rigid Calvinism and bald liturgy, were seldom renowned for tolerance or magnanimity, but Richard was an exceptional man among them; it was said of him, with some justification, that he was 'a man of sympathies so broad as to startle those of narrower persuasion'. During his early missionary years, spent in Shantung and Shansi, Richard travelled, listened, studied intensely until he was thoroughly conversant with every aspect of Chinese life and had developed a knowledgeable appreciation of Chinese culture. Others had done this before him but, unlike so many of them, Richard's approach to China was always open-hearted and open-minded. Influenced, undoubtedly, by the growth of Western interest in the comparative religions of the East, he constantly sought connections with which to build bridges between the great faiths of the world.

He studied the works of Islam and discussed them with the leaders of the Moslem communities that were numerous in western China; he was on sufficiently friendly terms with one prefectural governor to be invited to attend the opening of a new Confucian temple; he went to live among the Buddhists for a month and shared frugal meals and theological debate with the abbot of a Buddhist monastery. But he failed to gain the confidence of the local Taoist priests, grubby, saturnine men, each with a greasy tuft of hair poked through the crown of the black square hat atop their heads. So he wrote to the Taoist Pope asking for a sample of up-to-date writings on Taoism, and received in reply only some charms for the warding off of evil spirits.

During 1876 Richard was living in Ch'ung Chou, in Shantung, the first province to be badly affected by the famine which, it was estimated, killed fifteen million Chinese in three years and was one of the worst in recorded history. No rain fell to nourish the crops that first disastrous spring and the worried Chief Magistrate of Ch'ung Chou loaded himself with chains and walked barefoot to the temple to pray for rain, followed by crowds wearing chaplets of willow twigs and leaves. Richard, not to be outdone, 'rode forth on horseback like a son of the prophets', recorded his biographer, William Soothill, and pasted yellow placards on the city gates which stated that, if the people wanted rain, their only recourse was to turn from dead idols to the 'living God and pray unto Him and Obey his laws and conditions of Life'.

Soothill, writing in 1923, is faintly embarrassed by Richard's method and adds the ambiguous comment: 'Whether he expected God would miraculously intervene or not I do not know. In those days we all still believed in praying for rain, forgetful of our own past neglect, our wastefulness of the abundant supplies of the Divine Providence and the brains he had bestowed for development. Nevertheless it is perfectly true that people who worship dead idols do suffer vastly more than those who worship the living God, for idolatry is a mortmain upon the mind and heart, which are quickened into new life and activity under the spirit of the living God.' So Soothill tries to tease a meaning out of human suffering: it is permitted because of the praying Christian's own frailties; it must be inflicted upon the heathen because of their idolatry.

Either way, rain probably will not, and in Shantung during 1876 certainly did not, come. Yet Richard makes it clear in his own account that he *did* expect direct Divine intervention and that he firmly believed in its occurrence. As the period of drought lengthened he recorded that one of his converts 'led the representatives of thirty villages to pray to God for rain. Another time a woman led six of her neighbours to do the same, and it is my joy to record the fact that despite the sneers of sceptics, rain did fall in both instances.'

But it was never nearly enough, and Richard found it increasingly foolhardy to pit his God so bluntly against the powers of the native deities – for it seemed that no god of any creed or colour would have mercy on the shrivelled land. The rice of the next spring again shrank back into the cracked earth; the last of the village wells dried up and stank; the countryside was picked bone-clean by famine. 'The glowing sun is in the sky and locusts cover the ground,' wrote a lamenting Chinaman. 'There is no green grass in the fields and no smoke of cooking from the houses.' So skin-taut boys gnawed roots from the earth, elm bark from the trees and millet stalks from their own roof-thatch; rank weeds, thistles and the muddy husks scraped off the threshing floors of a richer time were chopped, boiled and eaten; the desperate women made 'cakes' from cotton seeds mixed with finely ground stones and these often caused constipation unto death. Men bartered all their farm implements for half a bowl of rice and tore down their door-posts and window frames for fuel, then they sold their daughters and lastly their wives.

Richard was one of the first missionaries to start a system of organised relief in Shantung, and it was so successful that the authorities asked him to go to Shansi, which was in an even worse plight because of the difficulties of transporting supplies inland. Richard went, travelling hundreds of miles by mule-cart through a ghoulish nightmare of suffering. The dying and the dead littered the roadsides, some being devoured by dogs, crows, magpies. Fat and fearless wolves prowled the villages watching for each new corpse as it fell – a weight become light enough for any flesh-filled wolf to drag away. Richard passed carts loaded with women and children who had been sold, and gaunt men skulking in alleyways armed with knives or spears. They needed the weapons for very literal self-protection. Murder and cannibalism were frighteningly common and it was rumoured that parents exchanged children in the market place because they could not endure to eat their own.

It was the coldest winter in the region for thirty years, the frozen Yellow River was solid enough for carts to cross it; 'the frozen ground yields nothing but pits for the dead', Richard wrote in his journal. And, 'saw six dead bodies in half a day, four of them women. One in the water half-exposed above the ice at the mercy of wild dogs; another half-eaten, torn by birds and beasts of prey. Met two youths of about eighteen years of age tottering on their feet and leaning on sticks as if they were ninety . . .'

Richard sent part of this laconic, dreadful journal to Shanghai and it was forwarded to London where it helped to stimulate contributions to the Lord Mayor's China Famine Relief Fund. Sizeable amounts of money were raised for the cause in Britain and America and missionaries of many societies joined in relief work. They lived in constant danger from the perils of bandits, wild animals, rioting mobs and 'famine fever', a form of typhus that often proved fatal; those who survived retained for life the searing memory of the scenes they had witnessed.

Timothy Richard, wrote Soothill, 'came out of the horror with the one word "education" branded upon his soul, a word which became the key-note of his life'. It might not seem the most obvious response, but the point was that Richard's efforts to get money and food distributed to the starving millions had brought him into close and frustrating contact with the gross inefficiencies of China's transport and communication systems and the inertia and obduracy of its authorities. He believed that many of the dead could have been saved 'if the Chinese officials had not been so full of pride, saying that they alone were civilised, that they alone had nothing to learn from the West'.

Thus the experience strengthened Richard's conviction that the only effective way to both Christianise and modernise China was first to try to enlighten the minds of government officials, professors, and other literati who were the crucial mainstays of its society. It was a strategy that he likened, in a somewhat dubious analogy, to the principle that, as water flows downhill more easily than it is pumped up, so truth will percolate more rapidly downwards from the top men in influential positions. The strategy, if not the analogy, had first been worked out by the Jesuits 250 years before, when they tried to use their knowledge of science and astronomy to make friends and influence people at the court of Peking.

To many Protestant missionaries therefore Richard's ideas smacked of Jesuitism and also suggested a sycophantic courting of the scholar and gentry class who embodied the proud culture and refined self-sufficiency of the Confucian ideal which was the natural enemy of Christianity. But Richard found much to admire both in the Confucian moral code and the writings of the early Catholic fathers, and was proud to acknowledge that he felt a great mental, as well as nominal, affinity with the brilliant Matteo Ricci. To those who accused him of evading his prime duty of direct Christian evangelism, he pointed out that there were many revered precedents for his methods. Had not the early Fathers of the Christian Church and the leaders of the Reformation, for instance, been men of affairs as well as of God? Education had ever been the ideal and pivot of Chinese civilisation and educated men the exemplars of its society, so what could be more efficacious than to gain their confidence first? Again, the principles and practice of modern Western science and philosophy would spread through China eventually in any case – and what more pernicious influence could there be than a godless arrogant science divorced from its background of Christian truth and morality?

So Richard proceeded to instruct himself in the latest advances of modern science. In 1879 he settled in T'ai-yuan, the capital of Shansi, where his work of famine relief had won him much good-will. He took with him his new wife, Mary, for he had 'come to the conclusion' that he could work more effectively as a married man. In the manner of most young missionaries announcing such a decision, he carefully avoided using words such as 'love', 'beauty' or 'sex' about his intended and lists instead her sensible, practical qualifications – which often makes missionary wives sound drearier than they probably were. So Mary was 'an accomplished lady of the United Presbyterian Mission' who 'had much experi-ence in education in the Merchant Company school in Edinburgh. She had been trained in theology under Dr Peddie and could more than hold her own in discussion with such a theologian as Gilmour of Mongolia. She is also gifted in music and leads in the musical part of our religious service.' Mary soon proved her worth to him. She organised an orphanage for sixty boys; translated improving stories into Chinese for her young pupils; learned so much about the native music that she once re-tuned all the instruments used in the nearby Confucian temple. She held enlightened views about women in society and was the first to draw attention to the parallel between Chinese foot-binding and Western waist-binding, berating her compatriot womenfolk for allowing themselves to be almost as much fashion's victims as the crippled Chinese ladies. She and Timothy both tried to teach the Chinese to value womanhood and when two daughters were born to them made special rejoicing over what was something of a disaster in native eyes.

The Richards lived frugally in their new home, for nearly all their money was spent on equipment for their education project: a telescope, microscope, spectroscope and a Wimhurst machine; induction coils, galvanometer, Geissler tubes and pocket sextant aneroids; a 'magic lantern worked by oxy-hydrogen' to show slides about how coffee and cocoa were grown; a sewing machine 'to show how one person could do the work of many'. Richard did not start the sort of Protestant mission school which was regarded with some scorn by the literati, but organised lectures in his own home on the physical sciences, medicine and mechanics of the West, and these proved very popular among the provincial officials and scholars.

He had no difficulty in reconciling his newly acquired knowledge with that of his vision of God as Rainmaker, because, for him, science was simply miracle revealed and his lectures bore such titles as 'The Miracle of Light as seen in the magic lantern and photography' and 'The astronomical Miracle as discovered by Copernicus'. The main burden of his theme was thus always the same: 'that we should study all the laws of God in Nature so as to gain the benefits that God intended to bestow upon us when He stored up all these forces for our use and then show our gratitude for all His loving-kindness by obeying His spiritual laws'. As he admitted in a letter, however, and as others had found before him, the great problem was how to 'lead these people from the study of these subjects in Nature up to Nature's God . . .'

Even setting aside the drastic metaphysical implications of this induction, Richard was up against the fact that the men he taught had been through a pedagogic mill which was not designed to prepare their minds for any kind of lead up or leap forward. As boys, their education had been almost entirely confined to the rote learning of Chinese history, classics and commentaries thereon; passages from these works were chanted aloud hour after hour and then repeated from memory to the teacher at his desk – a nerve-racking exercise called 'Backing the Books'. And many a traveller mentions that the discordant, incessant chorus of sixty boys yelling the wisdom of the sages at the top of their voices was, together with the grunt of hogs and the creak of wheels, the most characteristic medley of sounds in any Chinese village.

Any lad whose mind showed outstanding powers of retention and concentration then prepared for the first of the public examinations by perfecting his classical knowledge and learning to write essays and verses. Examinations in these skills were held at the District Magistrate's office, some lasting for five successive days. Survivors of these were summoned to the prefectural cities for examination by a literary chancellor; the successful at this stage coming through with literally flying colours – the academic blue

16 A contemporary Chinese anti-Christian poster showing the Devils (Europeans) worshipping the Incarnation of the Pig (the Lord)

17 The Return of the Prodigal Son, drawn by Matthew Tai, a Christian Chinese artist

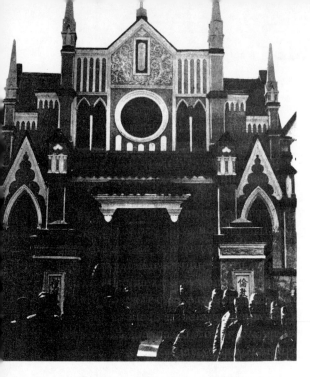

18 The London Missionary Society's central chapel at Hankow, with theological students and native evangelists in the foreground

19 A row of examination cells at the edge of an area containing about ten thousand such cells

20   A marketplace in Szechuan, photographed by Isabella Bird

21 A missionary on the road

22 Transport by wheelbarrow

silk robe and silver buttoned cap of the 'elegant scholar', the Chinese BA.

But, as for any BA, greater ordeals and rewards still loomed. Every year a public examination supervised by an imperially appointed commissioner was held in each provincial capital and thousands of elegant scholars journeyed from afar to sit for it. Not only sit but eat and sleep for it. The examination was held in a huge area which contained rows of up to ten thousand wooden cells, each measuring 5' 9" × 3' 8" and equipped with three trestle boards to serve as bench and desk by day and bed by night. Each candidate, supplied with food, brush pens and paper, was then sealed into a cell and left to write three 'eight-legged essays' and a poem on classical texts. He was there for two days and nights and it was none too long considering that each essay had to be written in eight formal, unalterable divisions and that a typical subject for one of them might be: 'Tzu-Kwong said to Confucius, "Suppose there were a man of such unbounded beneficence and power that he was able to extend help to every one of the people, what would you say to him? Might he be called humane?" Confucius answered, "Is humane the right word? Must he not be a holy man?"'

It must have been a considerable relief for the less able when the cell doors were unlocked and the candidates emerged weary-headed to a salutary roll of drums. The few who passed this stringent test were known as 'promoted men'; they swaggered back home wearing sea-green satin jackets, lavender shoes and hats with crimson tassels. Youths of any social rank, except the sons of jailors, executioners, scavengers – and actors! – were eligible for all examinations so that, in theory, the most mindful and diligent should have triumphed, but there was much abuse and some elegant scholars made an unenviable living by acting as substitutes for the less competent or smuggling cribs into the cells at night.

While the smugglers and substituters could be said to have shown a certain initiative, it was clear that the system did not encourage broadmindedness, flexibility or imagination. On the contrary, those in the higher echelons of officialdom were frequently bigotted, haughty men, obsessed with the niceties of etiquette and disinterested in the mundanities of provincial administration. Employment appropriate to their elevated rank was hard to find and their resulting sense of insecurity made them support the status quo with grim determination, fearful that any change would be to their detriment. In short such men were not malleable vessels for the reception of Christian truth, and Timothy Richard found that, in spite of his enterprising approach, his success rate among them was lower than that of the competitors in the examination cells.

But Richard never gave up. If he did not succeed at one level he was always ready to try a higher. Over the years he bombarded many of China's important and influential men with detailed schemes for technological development and modernisation. Why not open more mines and go into cotton manufacturing, he queried the Governor of Shantung? Why not build railways capable of carrying food supplies so that future famines could be avoided, he asked the Governor of Shansi (attaching an explanation of the Bessemer process of steel-making for the manufacture of rails)? Don't you see, he asked Viceroy Li Chang that if some foreign education was introduced throughout the country, the risk of war with foreigners would be greatly reduced? He corresponded with Sir Robert Hart and Sir Harry Parkes, the new British Minister, on these themes and later visited Peking to elaborate upon them in person, receiving quite a welcome from those who appreciated the breadth and originality of his outlook compared to most missionaries.

But not all; it would be wrong to suggest that Richard was alone in his views. Another who shared many of them was Dr W. A. P. Martin, a scholarly pioneer in the China mission field who had gone there in 1849; by the time Richard met him in the early 80s, he had been for twelve years President of the T'ung-wen College in Peking, founded by the Chinese for the advancement of Western studies. Martin was an American Presbyterian and American missionary societies were in the forefront of the movement to make higher Western-style education available to the people. Most of the first collegiate institutions in the treaty ports were

American and a number of promising young Chinese converts were sent for higher education in the States. However, many missionaries still felt that this sort of thing was outside the scope of their proper work and when Martin became President of the T'ung-wen he had to resign from the American Mission Board because no specific Christian instruction was permitted in the college's curriculum.

Martin justified his decision by the view he shared with Richard, that once the Chinese learned to appreciate the practical and social advantages of Western science and culture, they would naturally want the Christian faith as well. But he found, like Richard, that the native mind was fairly resistant. He tried to introduce it to the idea of the telegraph by having two sets of telegraphic instruments sent from America, and he invited some senior Peking officials to come and view the new miracle. They had a grand time, '. . . sending bell signals, wrapping copper wire about their bodies, breaking or closing the circuit and laughing heartily as they saw sparks leaping from wire to wire and setting hammers in motion'. But that was all; the telegraph was a novel toy and the officials didn't care to learn its operation or foresee its potential. So the telegraph ended up as lumber in the college museum and its main use was as an apt illustration, seized upon by later commentators, of the lamentable 'grooviness' of the Chinese.

Because of the catholicity and progressiveness of their activities during the 1860s and 70s, men like Richard and Martin raised issues about China's relationship to the outside world and to Christian culture which did not become common currency in missionary circles till years later. For Richard, like Martin, was eventually forced to sever his connection with the Baptists on account of his unconventional approach and both men were actually accused of heresy by some of their own colleagues. In the long run however, they were among the few missionaries to make a decisive individual impact on political and social opinion in China by their work as teachers, translators, innovators; in the late 90s, when their views had gained ground and their earlier warnings had crystallised into fact, they came into their own.

PART THREE

I have longed . . . to be of great service. When I was young — and very prideful — I was filled with a self-importance that . . . well disguised. That was the active word: I would serve! I would serve, and damn anyone or anything that stood in my way.

Edward Albee, TINY ALICE

CHAPTER NINE

God First

In the year 1882 Charles Darwin, who had opened and tormented so many of the best minds of his generation, died and was buried with full honours in Westminster Abbey. That same year the American evangelists, Dwight Moody and Ira Sankey, held a series of revivalist meetings at Cambridge University where some of the best minds of the next generation were under cultivation. Between those who mourned Darwin as founder of the new, honest, scientific rationalism and those who were deeply moved by the old-fashioned emotional oratory of the evangelists, the gulf was wide. It was a gulf of basic temperament and conviction that had caused much searing and widespread controversy during the previous twenty years; it was narrowed only by the healing idea that modern science was tool and reward bestowed by God upon worthy Christian nations to further their power and progress.

The temper of scientific humanism is now thoroughly defined and diffused among believers and non-believers alike, but in those days the grassroots religious spirit that nurtured the ordinary churchman remained almost untouched by it. When, in the gymnasium of the University, Moody denounced in doom-laden tones the failings of the prodigal son, many a young man hooted with derision, afterwards defiantly toasting his primordial apish ancestors with a sinful glass of porter; but there were others who, chilled by the cold comforts of Darwinism, stood up starry-eyed at the end of a crowded meeting to declare they had accepted

Christ and were determined upon the revival and reformation of their spiritual lives.

To this fervent need for dedication the American evangelists made enormous spontaneous appeal. They were dynamic central figures of the revivalist movement that had reached a peak during the 70s, when they made their first triumphal tour of Great Britain. This, their second coming, was not quite so successful, but they still needed the two portable iron tabernacles, each capable of holding up to five thousand people, which were erected on the outskirts of the big industrial cities that were their main rallying grounds. Even in London only the Agricultural Hall, Islington, and the Royal Opera House were large enough to accommodate all who flocked to hear their message. Dwight Moody was a stocky man from the New England backwoods who looked like a warehouse clerk and he preached on the theme of the narrow way to salvation through acceptance, repentance, regeneration. His material was earnest homespun: 'Look at Samson,' he implored his audience, 'when the spirit was on him how he worked! With the jaw-bone of an ass he slew a thousand men. People nowadays are not willing to work with the jaw-bone of an ass. They want some polished weapons that the world would not say anything against, but Samson came down from the rock and took up the first jaw-bone of an ass he came across and went and slew. . .' Moody's straight and narrow was made a little jollier with accompanying hymns composed by Ira Sankey which expressed in catchy informal manner the new spirit of militant cocksure Christianity. A favourite, for instance, was 'Hold the Fort', which began:

> Hold the Fort for I am coming,
> Jesus signals still;
> Wave the answer back to Heaven,
> By Thy grace I will.

Sankey, playing the cabinet organ, led fifteen-thousand-strong audiences in the choruses and the loops of gas-jets strung round the great public halls were set quivering with the lusty sound.

So vitalising was Moody's and Sankey's impact that they received a fairly cordial welcome from most religious denominations, though the higher Anglicans deplored their almost larrikin approach to the Most High and feared that the kind of fervour they aroused might easily degenerate into 'a mere sensualism'. But the evangelists' direct appeal for spontaneous, combative action awakened the idealistic conscience of hundreds of young people in Britain and America, among them a number of god-fearing, earnest students searching for a useful, worthy way of life. Some became unconventional clergymen working in the big-city slums; others, attuned to the outward-looking frontier spirit of imperialism, joined the ranks of overseas missionaries.

In Britain, the young man who most fully epitomized in the public mind the emotive ideal of rich, popular student turned devout, humble missionary was a certain Charles T. Studd. He was a Cambridge man, but as Charlie Studd or 'C. T.' he was widely known in non-academic circles for his prowess as a cricketer, and when Moody and Sankey visited the University in 1882, Charlie was in Australia helping England win the Ashes. During their earlier British tour however, the Americans had already made their presence very much felt in the Studd family. Edward, the father, had been a 'country gentleman who, after the services of Messrs Moody and Sankey, sold all his dogs and hunters and devoted himself to Christian work', as a missionary pamphlet explained, and he had then tried to recruit all his offspring under the same banner. 'It did make one's hair stand on end,' Charlie later recalled, 'how everyone in the house had a dog's life of it until they were converted. . . He used to come into my room late at night and ask if I was converted.' The urgent aggressiveness of Edward Studd's method was typical, for most of Moody's converts became premillenniumists who believed in the imminence of the world's destruction and Christ's second coming. Consequently salvation was an urgent matter that could not be postponed until the next, and always possibly the last, day.

For years 'C. T.' resisted parental pressure and remained, in his own words, 'a merely lisping Christian' more concerned with his hero-size reputation on the cricket field. Then the near-fatal illness of a beloved brother renewed his halting faith; he actively supported the Moody campaign in its last year, 1884, and then committed his future entirely 'to Christ'. It was an intense decision that gave him great joy and he described it thus: 'I had formerly as much love for cricket as any man could have, but when the Lord Jesus came into my heart I found that I had something infinitely better than cricket. My heart was no longer in the game. I wanted to win souls for the Lord. I knew that cricket would not last and honour would not last and nothing in the world would last; but it was worthwhile living for the world to come.'

Studd spoke those simple words on a pouring wet evening in February 1885 before 3,500 people in Exeter Hall along London's Strand. They had come, despite the weather, to hear the testimonies of seven young men already celebrated as The Cambridge Seven, who had volunteered for service as China Inland Mission members. Studd of course was one, and another was Arthur Polhill-Turner who had planned a conventional life as clergyman of the family living in rural Bedfordshire until Moody's call beckoned him to sterner pastures. Arthur's elder brother Cecil resigned a coveted commission in the Dragoon Guards to join the Seven and another recruit from the army was Dixon Hoste, a general's son. Hoste experienced sudden, definite conversion during one of the revivalists' meetings and always recalled his first sight of the man who changed the course of his life. 'He was dressed in a business suit and had nothing of the customary clerical appearance about him. From the minute he stepped on the platform my eyes involuntarily followed his every movement. This was Mr Moody; there could be no mistake. There was something about him that was different.' The rest of the Seven comprised William Cassels, a merchant's son and an ordained clergyman, Stanley Smith, son of a surgeon and former Captain of the Cambridge Eight, and Montagu Beauchamp, son of that same Sir Thomas who had, some twenty years before, responded with only apparent recklessness to Hudson Taylor's appeal for funds by giving him the insurance premium for his conservatories.

Now at last it seemed that all Taylor's prayerful appeals were bearing fruit that full-fed his boldest expectations. The seven young men were all endowed with money, social standing and athletic prowess and would greatly enhance the Mission's reputation; Taylor, with his flair for publicity, made the most of their recruitment. The Exeter Hall meeting opened with a wholehearted rendering of 'Tell it out among the Heathen that the Lord is King' and then each of the Seven rose to explain his personal reasons for joining the CIM. It was a drastic and seemingly improvident step for any young person to take, but what so captured the imagination of the public about the Seven was the extent of their sacrifice.

It was arguable that the spinster daughter of a Midlands shopkeeper, for example, might gain more from life simply in the secular terms of marriage opportunity, social standing and sheer interest by going overseas as a missionary. But these young men were, as one speaker said, '. . . putting aside the splendid prizes of earthly ambition which they might reasonably have expected to gain, taking leave of the social circles in which they shone with no mean brilliance and plunging into the warfare whose splendours are seen only by faith and whose rewards seem so shadowy to the unopened vision of ordinary men'.

Of the Seven, Stanley Smith was endowed with the greatest eloquence, and all were moved by the sight of 'the big muscular hands and long arms of the ex-Captain of the Cambridge Eight stretched out in entreaty while he told the old story of Redeeming Love. . .' Smith reminded his audience that the Apostles were not content to preach 'the milk and water of religion but the cream of the Gospel' to the heathen and that they too, the Seven, were taking nothing but the best 'to the Chinaman buried in theories and prejudices and bound by chains of lust'. Cassels reminded everyone of the pressing need for more 'to come forward and join in the warfare'. Had they not all read of Reuben who stayed to look after his sheep instead of going to battle? Of Gilead who wouldn't risk crossing the Jordan? Of Dan engaged in his own commerce? People stirred uneasily, were perhaps relieved when the sober cleric sat down and made way for dear old Charlie Studd, who was not much of an orator but who only had to be there to be loved. The Reverend C. Searle summed up popular sentiment about him afterwards when he wrote, 'We who can recollect the strong man, how great he would rise with his bat, with what force he would hurl his ball, how grand the ovation he would receive as Captain of the victorious, we who knew how such a man is sought out, caressed and idolised, can in some measure estimate his sacrifice, or rather the strength of the new force that laid hold of him.'

So between them the Seven presented to their admirers the very apotheosis of muscular Christianity – buoyant, manly, straight-forward and with that combination of unquestioning social assurance and uncomplicated devoutness that the Victorians loved. In case the message of the Seven was not clear enough, the Reverend Price Hughes, a well-known non-conformist, spelled it out with rather startling honesty during his final address: 'Thank God for men picked up by the Salvation Army – from the gutter too, some of them – who are setting an example of bravery which may God help us to follow; but when you have this grand enthusiasm combined with culture and social position, how much more glorious it is!'

The morning after the meeting admiring crowds gathered at Victoria Station to cheer the little band on its way and to note that earnest, unobtrusive William Cassels had the words 'God First' printed in large red capitals on all his heavy luggage. As the Seven sailed towards Heathendom religious publications in Britain vied with each other in their enthusiastic accounts. The Secretary of the Church Missionary Society, though he would have dearly loved such recruits, generously said that 'no event of the century had done so much to rouse the minds of Christian men to the tremendous claims of the field and the nobility of the missionary vocation'. Another writer went so far as to liken the Seven to the original apostolic twelve for their spiritual zeal and singleminded-ness – and certainly their voluntary sacrifice of so many worldly goods and joys made the forsaking of a few boats and fishing nets seem quite pale by comparison.

A full report of the Exeter Hall meeting was printed in the next issue of *China's Millions* and over fifty thousand copies of it were sold. This CIM magazine was unusually successful and its separate issues appeared annually in bound volumes. It was probably Hudson Taylor himself who recognised their appeal as coffee-table books. Wrote a reviewer of one volume: 'It is beautifully, almost sumptuously bound and if placed on the drawing-room table will excite an interest that a more modest cover would probably fail to arouse. . .'

The tidal wave of enthusiasm and acclaim which the Seven had aroused still lapped about them when they reached China, and there, buoyed high themselves, they re-invigorated the zeal of others. At Shanghai they held a 'Meeting for the Deepening of the Spiritual Life' in the Temperance Hall during which the resident British Chaplain himself was moved to 'confess anew to Christ', saying he had never before been 'a fully committed soul'. From Shanghai, Hoste, Cassels and Smith went to Peking where the impassioned speeches of the latter stirred the hearts of many resident missionaries. 'Only twenty-four years old and burning with the zeal and eloquence of a Xavier,' wrote one, and Dr Edkins felt that their coming was 'as a salutary purifying breeze . . . The crust of conventional precedent and reluctance has been broken through at our meetings with them and the tongues of those who have blessed have been set free to speak of God's goodness.'

The American missionaries were no less enchanted and one, the Reverend E. Blodget, wrote an account of their stay for the New York *Independent*. 'Their lives are marked by self-denial, prayer and fasting. They visited no remarkable places in Peking, saw no sights, wondered at nothing, but made it their one object while here to seek for themselves and for Christians the power of God's Spirit according to His Promise.' Blodget's tone is genuinely admiring, but how it diminishes them now – that such educated, energetic young men who had never before set foot beyond Suez should stay for two months in the capital of one of the world's most colourful, sophisticated cultures and wonder at *nothing*. How insular they were, arrogantly hidebound by the moral imperatives and exclusive judgements of their narrow faith.

But secure within its limits the Seven remained full of joy and confidence during their early time in China. 'My all is on the altar. The fire is come. He has given me a clean heart, Hallelujah!' ran one of Smith's first postcards home. 'It is a very honeymoon time with the Lord in a quiet cool place,' wrote C. T. of his first stay in a Chinese village. They began to familiarise themselves with the country by rural itinerations, earnestly pressing their tracts upon the sullen-eyed or curious and then, mounting some vantage point of market stall or buffalo cart, they stuttered out their first exhortations in halting Chinese. It was amazing how little hostility they met, considering that their behaviour was as reckless and impudent as if 'a Chinese Buddhist mounting the roof of a hansom cab at Charing Cross had preached of Buddhism in pidgin English', as one critic pointed out in a fair analogy.

While yearning for the gift of tongues, the young men channelled their pent-up fervours into letters crammed with the Bible-saturated shorthand which circulated, talisman-like, among missionaries. 'I have got such a blessing lately over Rom. vi and Ephes. ii,' wrote Smith from P'ing yang fu. 'We are very happy in soul,' reported Dixon Hoste, 'though we have not yet had much scope for the happiness of James V. ii.' This, the happiness of the Stoic that results from the patient, strong endurance of prolonged grief or difficulty, was the mettle they longed to test themselves upon. 'We despair almost of having any hardships or meeting with any discomforts, for things get brighter and brighter and at every turn more and more comfortable,' Cassels complained in a letter home. And Charles Studd, realising that his life was still cushioned by the fortunate circumstances of his birth and upbringing, divested himself with dramatic thoroughness of all his former assets. When travelling by water he used to squat in the bow with the boatmen and share their simple meals; when sitting he preferred a wooden stool without a back (scorning the 'armchair Christians' ensconced at home); when he inherited £25,000 he gave it away to charity. He and his wife Priscilla ('a real Salvation Army Hallelujah lassie', as C. T. described her), were agreed on this and wrote a joint letter home to explain their decision. 'Henceforth our bank is in Heaven. You see we are rather afraid – notwithstanding the great earthly safety of Messrs Coutts & Co and the Bank of England – we are, I say, rather afraid that they may both break on the Judgement Day, and this step has been taken not without most definite reference to God's word and the command of Lord Jesus who said, "Sell all ye have and

give alms. Make for yourself purses which wax not old . . ."'
From then on the Studds depended, as did their colleagues, on the
uncertain arrival of scant funds from well-wishers. For, as the CIM
'Arrangements' of the 1880s stated, no fixed salaries were guaran-
teed and each member was 'expected to recognise that his dependence for the supply of his need is on God who called him and for
whom he has gone to labour, and not on the human organisation'.
So Charles and Priscilla were often practically, though never
completely, penniless, but it did not matter anyway, for they
felt themselves to be 'spiritual millionaires'.

The supreme confidence of the Studds' gesture was typical of
the Seven's spirit in their early days when they were cast on a
somewhat heroic scale. They talked breezily of 'attacking' villages
with posters, Bibles and paste-pots and of 'the Evil One round
about us as a roaring lion', whom they, the Christian knights in
armour clad, would soon be ready to take on in dangerous,
single-handed combat. It was psychologically sound, for people
so brimful of faith found constant stimulus in the stress of 'battle
conditions', as did their leader. Taylor enacted a personal lifelong
drama on this theme and his letters are full of references to it:
'Satan is so busy just now! There is trial on every hand . . . The
conflict is heavy indeed and Satan harasses on all sides . . .'

However, in the longer term the Seven had to face the fact that
the attempt to Christianise China was not comparable to an
action-packed invasion by an expeditionary force. And this was
the hardest lesson for them to learn, after the acclamatory tide
that had marked their arrival finally ebbed and they were posted
to various inland mission stations to cope with less glorious and
pedestrian enemies such as loneliness, frustration, apathy and
disappointment.

CHAPTER TEN

The Smooth and the Rough

William Cassels, the only member of the Seven with previous experience of evangelism – as a curate in the London slums – was the first to open his own mission station. An Anglican clergyman and member of the Church Missionary Society as well as the China Inland Mission, Cassels was clearly on the establishment side of the Protestant spectrum. The CIM was predominantly non-conformist and, to try and avoid doctrinal disputes, Hudson Taylor's policy was to allocate separate areas to each denomination substantially represented in his Mission. Thus Cassels was 'given' Szechuan, a province of some sixty-eight million people, almost as large as France; it stretched westwards to the Tibetan frontier and was so habitually cloudy that, according to a native saying, dogs barked when they saw the sun appear there.

Cassels saw his task as being 'to build up a work there within the CIM that is loyal and consistent with Church of England principles', and he devoted his life to it. He spent a total of thirty-eight years in Szechuan and died there in 1925, still 'girt in full armour in the midst of his grand work', as Cecil Polhill-Turner expressed it. With the armour brand-new and shining and no thought of defeat or death, Cassels set out for Szechuan in the autumn of 1886. His first sight of it was from the summit of an 'arduous peak', the chosen land lying below, shrouded in cloud as usual. Then suddenly, as he looked, the sun burst through and the words of Isaiah illuminated him: 'Arise shine, for Thy light is come and the glory of the Lord is risen upon thee. For behold, the darkness shall cover the earth and gross darkness the people; but the Lord shall arise upon thee and His Glory shall be seen upon thee . . .'

Cassels chose for headquarters Paoning, the 'City of Assured Peace', the dignified prefectural capital, with some forty thousand generally peaceable inhabitants. It was so dependent on its main trade of silk that, in early summer, the local women used to carry the cocoons about in the warm place between their clothes and their breasts to ensure a good hatching. There were side-lines – the steaming of bread, expert treating of pigs' bristle, spicing of pork, pressing of oil from the seeds of the wood-oil tree used in the waterproofing of a million crackly paper umbrellas – but the general pace was leisurely and cultured.

The city had famous Buddhist and Confucian temples, a mosque for the numerous Moslems, a special shrine for the Goddess of Disease whose festival was celebrated in the fifth month, an examination area filled with wooden cells. 'Elegant scholars' who had retired or grown tired of writing essays dwelt in rambling residences in the suburbs whose courtyards were shaded with peach, fig and mulberry. Lanes bordered with wild limes meandered away to the surrounding countryside where even the farm servants who, as the saying went, 'lived with their backs to the sky and their faces to the mud', were allowed to straighten up more than most of their oppressed kind.

Cassels bustled about the city with enormous, impatient vigour. He was eventually allowed to rent a house, though the yamen magistrate was understandably reluctant to accept the consequent responsibility for the Mission's protection. Then followed the usual business of repairing and furnishing the new compound, though Cassels, aching 'to see souls won', grudged the time spent on such mundanities. 'For myself I know there is a great unsatisfied gap in my heart when I lay down at night after spending the day arranging furniture, curtains, pictures, etc. I can't testify to feelings of joy, though it may be ever so necessary to have these things, may all be done to the glory of God . . .' But a wife must be provided with a chair and table – for William had decided to marry one Mary Louisa, after and in spite of his original decision to remain in a state of Pauline celibacy. He justified his change of heart on the grounds that, if he had not made it, Mary would have been so very deeply wounded that he wouldn't dare be responsible for the consequences. Poor Cassels! Like so many an ardent devout young missionary, he set himself impossibly high standards of spiritual, practical and emotional attainment, and so spent many weary hours in fasting, praying and 'deeper self-questionings', writhing at the 'new depths' of his own iniquities and frequently appalled by the occasional frailty of the flesh, limitation of the mind, dryness of the spirit.

However, after his marriage Cassels began to learn to live with his lot. He created a hive of Christian activity at Paoning which was typical of many inland mission stations. Isabella Bird, the traveller, visited it in the early 90s, by which time it had become an extensive collection of '. . . humble Chinese houses built round two compounds in which two married couples, three bachelors and, in the Bishop's House [Cassels was by then Bishop of Western China], two ladies were living and, at some distance off, there is the ladies' house occupied by five ladies. There are several guest-halls for Chinese visitors, class and school rooms, porters' and servants' rooms. The furniture is all Chinese and the whitewashed walls are decorated with Chinese scrolls chiefly . . .'

Though 'humble' enough in Western eyes, such stations offered a sense of cleanly order and seclusion that was far removed from the workaday streets outside, with their constant throb of human jostle – pedlars selling everything from embroidery thread to caged squirrels, children playing 'Pass the Seed' or 'Water Demon Seeking Den', yamen runners roughly clearing the way for the loftily swaying official's chair. The noise of it all, muted, drifted over the high mission walls to the main courtyard where peonies, lilac, hibiscus bloomed; in the 'farm courtyard' at the back other colours shone – black sheen of a mortar where golden cracked wheat was pounded, deep-green glaze of storage jars filled with a purplish mush of sorghum and soya, white doves nestling under grey-tiled eaves. Silence, that most expensive of Chinese luxuries, was broken only by the doves cooing, slip-slop of maid's sandals as she went to hang the buffalo butter in the well to keep cool, rustle of nursemaid braiding a little basket in the sun, leisurely scrape of gatekeeper's broom, notes of an harmonium as the missionary's wife practised the hymns for Sunday.

Thus anchored and enclosed the missionaries evolved their rounds of duties and rituals. The day began about seven with prayers in the chapel; after breakfast the missionaries spoke informally about the Gospel to any potential enquirers within range – patients waiting in the dispensary, addicts in the opium refuge, carpenters doing repairs, hawkers bringing vegetables, washerwomen, shoemenders, and people who just called out of curiosity. During the day the missionaries held classes for enquirers, native evangelists, colporteurs and Bible women. Most missions had their own Manuals of Instruction, supplemented by simply-worded pamphlets such as 'Old Mrs Wrinkles and the Questions she asked about Jesus'. Also, there were always converts with problems to sort out. It might be the relatively simple matter of Mrs Tsui's baby boy who had just died of smallpox and Mrs Tsui's wanting to know how God could have permitted this when she had been a diligent church-attender for a year. Or it was the pathetic case of the peasant Eng-teh Dzing with six daughters, no sons and a recently failed harvest, who was sorely tempted to sell 'Little-fat-number three' child to a 'devil granny' in the brothel quarter – even if it did mean his expulsion from the Church. Mr Wong the bucket-maker also had a daughter, formerly betrothed to a 'heathen', and when the Wongs became Christians she had obeyed the missionaries' instructions and broken the engagement. But such flouting of a legal, sacrosanct contract aroused the hostility of the whole neighbourhood and now no one would give Mr Wong orders for bucket-making and the jilted son's family had secretly set fire to his bean patch and killed his three pigs, so that the family were almost starving. Naturally, Mr Wong felt the missionaries now had a duty to provide him with a livelihood, and didn't they need a third assistant gatekeeper . . .? As dusk fell, the missionaries, wearied by the endless sharp clack of Chinese voices in dispute, retired to their rooms for an hour of private meditation before evening prayers and supper. Gongs announced the closing of the city gates, the Mission's pallid children were put to bed by the amahs, the beggar outside the compound gate began his nightly keening, the animals in the farm-court brayed for their evening meal and were fed by Mr Wong, the new fourth stable-hand.

This outline routine of inland mission life remained constant over the years, usually directed by resident senior missionaries such as William Cassels, while other personnel kept moving about – the lay term for the CIM was 'Constantly In Motion'. Bachelors and single ladies, though so carefully placed in very separate quarters as Isabella Bird stresses, still married each other quite frequently and went off to open 'out-stations' of their own. Pairs of spinsters were posted to quiet places off the beaten track to work among the elderly or the Buddhist 'vegetarian women' who were, in Cassels' opinion, 'often easily won over and zealous in spreading the truth'. Larger, more important plums were the male preserve: 'As for Shanking,' Cassels wrote to his Committee, 'I think you will agree that a big place like that will need brethren's work. May the Lord soon send brethren to us.'

Any newly arrived brother not yet fluent in the language could, Cassels added, be 'usefully employed in drawing crowds for the native evangelists if he sings or is willing to be a "sign-board"'. He could also be put to work on the growing volume of administration such as the keeping of wages and expenditure accounts and the literal dividing of financial resources. Money came upcountry in fist-size, 5-lb silver ingots called 'shoes', and they had to be taken to a smithy where they were fired, beaten into thin slabs, then cut into tiny square bits for distribution.

Another mission chore was the collection of mail from out-stations, its onward transmission, and the distribution of mail from home – and that was important for morale, when the absence of home-letters was called a 'fast', their arrival a 'feast'. The home-based missionary societies also helped to keep up morale by the circulation of their magazines which were treasuries of uplifting anecdotes and success stories. The one about Mrs Uen, for instance, who whitewashed her whole house after her conversion 'lest the Lord when He came should be grieved by the lingering odour of incense which she used to burn to her ancestral idols'; the one about keen young Lo Fan who, when grinding corn, propped a hymn book against a stone and 'as he watched the buffalo plodding round was also learning his favourite hymn, "Onward Go"'.

Reports of conferences past and agendas for those to come also needed organising and circulating, for so much had to be decided in conference as missionary numbers increased. There were committees for assessing language ability, arranging the training of native agents, allocating internal funds (should the available money go towards the supply of Tobin's Best Ventilation Tubes for the hospital or the Calorigen stove needed in the single ladies' chilly sitting-room?) and for deciding other personal priorities – Mr Simmonds had constant toothache and begged leave to go to a Shanghai dentist; Mr Knight's wife was expecting her first and begged for her husband's escort to the coast; they couldn't both be spared at once.

Problems of larger implication also came up, as, for instance, before Paoning Fu Native Church Council Meeting, held at Wong-shao on the 18th and 19th of October, 1888, also the 14th Year of the Kwong-ju, 3rd and 4th days of the ninth month. The stickiest item on the agenda was the Reverend Sing Eng-tiu's application for official missionary support against the headman of his village who had demanded that the Christians living there should pay the customary tax used to finance the local 'heathen festivals'. By the terms of the 1860 treaties, converts were legally exempt from such taxes, but exemptions were hard to enforce unless there was a missionary on the spot; for refusal to pay often resulted in persecution which took colourful oriental forms like the cutting off of a convert's ears, hanging him from a tree by his pigtail, castrating his hogs or daubing his kitchen with night-soil. So in this case Cassels prudently refused to interfere on the Reverend's behalf and requested instead that the pastor exhort his little flock to patient endurance of any trials 'as they are called upon to suffer and to remind them of the examples of early Christians as recorded in the New Testament'.

While some missionaries unquestioningly accepted the comparatively secure rhythms of mission-station life, others began to feel that it was somewhat remote from the trials that converts were 'called upon to suffer' and even more so from the millions who never came anywhere near a mission. One who expressed the latter view very vocally and plagued Cassels and his superiors with it for years was the Reverend Heywood Horsburgh, another Cambridge man, a prickly tense ascetic whose mind was in constant emotional and spiritual turmoil. He arrived in China with his delicate wife Adelaide and a sickly daughter just before the Cambridge Seven; but he was a CMS man and so came under the supervision of George Moule, now Bishop of Mid-China, and Arthur, now an archdeacon in his brother's diocese.

Twenty-five years' living in China had not changed either Moule very much (their name was fortuitous). Arthur, weighed down with secretarial administration in Shanghai, found it pleasurably nostalgic to ride out from the city in a jinrikisha on summer nights to preach in a street chapel, or to take an itineration through the surrounding countryside, armed with a leather satchel stuffed with tracts. He had perfected his own methods of proselytism, as his biographer explained. One was to join on the end of a line of peasants as they wended single-file across the narrow paddy paths, and then, 'lifting his voice like a Chinaman so that the whole line could hear, he would join in the conversation, leading it from crops and markets, or from landscape and sky quickly to the great theme. When the party came to a rest-shed, he would seat himself and speak to those seated there, quoting perhaps his favourite proverb that "though the rest-shed be good it is no abiding home", and so go on to speak of the Life Beyond and the Heavenly Home.' Arthur, his biographer adds, always climbed every hill because he loved to preach from summits. So much energy and effort of their most creative years had the Moule brothers now invested in their chosen field that they could no longer afford to admit failure; but Arthur, making one of his depressingly honest reviews a few years later, reckoned that thirty years of missionary work in Chekiang province had brought a total of two thousand converts, which was considerably less than one in every ten thousand inhabitants.

Heywood Horsburgh, bleakly confronted with this seeming inefficacy of the Word, assumed, as others before him, that the fault must lie in the evangelistic methods used. Within a few weeks he was out in the streets '. . . to sell tracts and stammer about his beloved Lord', wrote Arthur Moule, in the tart tones he began to adopt when describing Horsburgh's activities. For Moule soon recognised in the prickly newcomer that reckless, innovatory spirit of the 'enthusiast' which had galvanised Hudson Taylor twenty years before and caused such trouble. For though Horsburgh, Moule continued in a later letter, was indeed possessed of a 'noble sense of spirit', he was 'as is the case of many other heavenly-minded people, strangely obstinate and opinionated. His experience is very brief and very limited, but he allows it to override the opinion of those who have been ten times as long in the field . . .'   .

Moreover, Horsburgh's 'strangely obstinate' opinion was similar to Taylor's: that Christianity, known among the Chinese as 'the foreigners' religion', must be divorced from its Western background and taught 'along simple apostolic lines'. 'We who preach and practise it are surrounded by foreign-style trappings and these must be stripped away,' he told his Home Committee, emphasising the strength of his conviction with three underlinings per word. But to try and strip away from long-established, church-oriented missionaries of the CMS like the Moules such trappings as they had accumulated, justified, become unquestioningly accustomed to over the years, was like trying to peel an ancient oak-tree with a blunt pen-knife.

Still Horsburgh was a trier, and his first step was to return a proportion of his salary to the Society, saying that he and his family could manage on less and suggesting that his colleagues could do likewise if they practised a few economies. Why, for instance, did all the ladies need to transport 'forty or fifty boxes of stuff each' up to an inland station, at considerable expense and thus exciting the envy, curiosity and greed of the natives? Why didn't the mission families sack a few servants, or sell the children's pony, or travel second-class instead of first? What about putting a general 'Do-Without Box' in every dining-room? Couldn't they all see that the resultant savings would finance the sending of more missionaries to the field, and that surely was the top priority? This put rather on the spot a number of comfortably-ensconced treaty-port missionaries, and Arthur Moule did indeed return some of his salary to the Society, 'but *not*,' he protested in the accompanying letter, 'because it is any larger than I honestly require.' Archibald Moule, Arthur's student-missionary son, did his bit of 'roughing it' by travelling to England second class. He was, however, obliged to report to his father that though the food was just edible, his second-class travelling companions were 'most objectionable' and there was 'only one gentleman among them ...'

'Roughing it' means different things to different people. Some of Horsburgh's brethren found his proud asceticism as embarrassing and conscience-pricking as the offer of an actual hair shirt; others were goaded into justification of the opposite standpoint. One of the latter was the Reverend B. G. Henry who worked for ten years in Canton and lamented that, in earlier days, 'missionaries had been compelled to live in native houses where they suffered greatly from dampness and want of proper drainage besides many other evils and discomforts; while in the matter of food and furniture the rigid economy practised proved most expensive in the end. The seeds of disease were laid and strong constitutions undermined ... With experience came wisdom and most mission-aries are now found in airy, substantial and comfortable houses ...' This, Henry concluded, is correct, for, 'to secure the respect of the people it is necessary to assume a proper dignity and appear to them as people of assured social position and refinement. Any attempt to bring ourselves down to a level with the masses would simply destroy the influence naturally belonging to one's position and expose oneself to innumerable petty annoyances.'

Horsburgh, reading that, would have gone rage-purple and demanded to know what concern Christ showed for his 'social position' and the 'petty annoyances' inflicted by the masses? Perhaps he did read it; certainly at the Mid-China Conference of 1887 he produced detailed accounts to show how he and his family lived reasonably well with one servant in a native house on two-thirds of their salary and challenged all present to say why and for what they needed more. Was it to give their children an expensive education? To provide such luxuries as bathrooms, private rickshaws, holidays by the sea? Should not missionaries 'lay aside all ambition for themselves and their children as far as money is concerned'? He sent his accounts and a report of his challenging speech to Salisbury Square, adding in red ink at the bottom: 'NB. That challenge still stands and has not yet been satisfactorily answered'.

To members of the Committee, well cushioned by distance from the scenes of dispute, Horsburgh's approach sounded original and enterprising, and, hampered as they were by shortage of funds, they felt that the 'idea of conducting missionary operations on a less expensive system' had much to recommend it. So when Horsburgh wrote to ask if he could begin working away from the over-staffed, over-civilised coastal areas, his request was granted. The Moules, George, Arthur, their wives, sons, nephews all living in the treaty ports, were furious. The dispute was a logical extension of the differences of principle and strategy that had emerged from the China Inland Mission fracas of the 1860s, but it was more complex because missionaries were much more firmly entrenched in their positions and because this was a viper-in-the-bosom affair with Horsburgh, a CMS man, getting support from the people at headquarters. 'I have grave apprehensions as to the suitability of our good brother for such a vast yet vague enterprise,' Arthur wrote to them, in that tone of windy fore-boding of which he had long been master. He went on to accuse the Committee of allowing Horsburgh 'to put into action principles which condemn in the simplest possible way the methods adopted for forty years in the Society's China Mission and which God has owned by His approving seal'. Both brothers were doubly stung because their diocesan authority had been over-ruled. 'We are very tempted to think,' Bishop Moule bitingly remarked, 'that views find favour in Salisbury Square in proportion to the scantiness of their support in China.'

But to a man of Horsburgh's stamp, controversy was a spur and the opposition of colleagues proof of his own God-given sense of rightness. So he put on his own peculiar version of a Chinese-style 'travelling dress' ('he was more afraid of a frock coat and the rest of the English outfit than of all the devils of the evening,' snarled one of his critics) and walked three hundred miles to the western provinces, where he hoped to work in easier accord with members of the CIM. On arrival he travelled for a while with Monty Beauchamp, who had become the itinerator par excellence of the Cambridge Seven, having clocked up no less than 1,500 miles of continuous tramp with bundles of tracts slung on a pole over his shoulder. But Horsburgh's frail physique was not up to this and he suffered recurrent breakdowns and fevers – caused, his detractors said, by the instability of his temperament and the unhealthy native style of his living. After nearly two years that were notable only for the quantity of his theories and the paucity of his practice, Horsburgh determined to concentrate his efforts on Szechuan and thus came under the nominal authority of William Cassels.

Cassels had always been the most church-oriented of the Seven. He wore a surplice in church; one of his main ambitions was to train for ordination some native pastors and deacons who would be 'capable of the meaningful administration of the sacraments'. He was proud of the exclusive moral and doctrinal standards he maintained in the Paoning Fu Mission and his years of diligent, cautious work had allayed the earlier 'serious misgivings' that Bishop Moule 'had been forced to entertain' about his connection with the CIM. The inevitable disagreements that therefore arose between Cassels and Horsburgh reflected the divisions in the Anglican Church. Just as clergymen from 'high' sophisticated London town argued with their colleagues from 'low' rural Lancashire about whether the choir need be adorned with surplices and the altar with tall candles, so in Szechuan, Horsburgh accused Cassels of 'choking the simple ignorant people with rites and ceremonies', or burdening them with sectarianism by 'setting up a lot of little C. of E.'s . . . with pews, vestments and other needless churchy accoutrements'. The most absurd instance of this, incidentally, was that CMS missionaries carried loaves of stale, foreign-made bread and watered-down claret on their itinerations in order to offer a correct administration of the sacraments – and this in a mainly bread-less and wine-less country. One CMS man was bold enough to suggest the substitution of tea and rice-cake, but such a suggestion was vetoed because of its wide implications. Cassels would have been among the vetoers, for what other Church could they offer but their own C. of E. he asked irritably? So Horsburgh wanted to add chaos to the present sectarian confusion 'by the creation of a Horsburgh sect, the no-sect-sect'? Hmm? Hmm?

It did come to that eventually, but first Horsburgh spent another two years with the CMS travelling through the interiors in a leaky house-boat called the *Advance*. Lost to foreign sight for months on end ('Where *is* Horsburgh?' Cassels plaintively enquired of the Home Committee on at least three occasions. 'Do *you* know?') he preached and distributed tracts to the thousands who lived along and on the great rivers. In the evenings, squatting in the boat's bow, he scribbled reams of scarcely-legible justification for his ever-changing views. 'My engagements are far too numerous for me to attempt to follow my dear brother in all his lengthy effusions,' Cassels told his superiors, after the receipt of a particularly thick missive. The one factor that remained constant through all Horsburgh's writing and speaking was his sense of divinely-inspired rightness and intimate personal link with God. 'I am certain it is not God's will for me to learn an entirely new provincial dialect at this time,' he informed the Committee who had suggested his leaving Szechuan to Cassels and moving on to less-tilled fields. It was a recourse that stymied his superiors in England, while those in China found it insufferable. 'His mixture of devout humility of the spirit with an obstinacy on practical questions that does the work of self-confidence makes discussion with him discouraging,' was one of Arthur's cooler descriptions of it.

After a last bout of mutually painful quarrels with the Moules, Horsburgh started his own radical offshoot of the CMS in 1891. He called it the Mid-China Interior Evangelisation Mission and gathered under its banner several other young missionaries who were attracted by the bright fires of his pure idealism. They managed to 'obtain a foothold' in six Szechuan cities previously 'unopened'; one of them was Kuan Hsien, where the almost equally peripatetic Isabella Bird came upon Horsburgh and his ever-loving Adelaide in 1896. She photographed Horsburgh in his stained, tattered 'travelling dress' and wrote an objective description of their actual mode of living. Their temporary lodgings were in a foul alley, '. . . dirty, broken, half the paper torn off the windows and eaves so deep and low that daylight could scarcely enter. There was an open guest-hall used constantly for classes and services; endless parties of Chinese passed in and out all day long, poking holes in the remaining windows, opening every door that was not locked, taking everything they could lay hands on; the noise was only stilled from 4 to 6 a.m. – men shouting, babies screaming, dogs barking, squibs and crackers going off and drums beating – no rest, quiet or privacy. There are two services in the guest-hall on Sunday conducted by Mr Horsburgh, superintendent of the Mission, and several classes for women also, but all in a distracting babel – men playing cards outside the throng, men and women sitting for a few minutes, some laughing scornfully, others talking in loud tones, some lighting their pipes, a very few really interested. This is not the work which many who go out as missionaries on a wave of enthusiasm expect, but this is what these good people undergo, day after day, month after month . . .'

And year after year like that, and wherever they went 'very few really interested'. No wonder that Horsburgh became ever more austere and tense, ever more isolated and melancholy, unstable to the point of madness some said, and certainly the light of the fanatic must have shone in his eyes. A similar light, his supporters felt, that surely shone from the eyes of Horsburgh's Master and, paradoxically, a light that could not but threaten those few tangible gains which Cassels and the Moules had so painfully wrought from the solid rock of Chinese indifference.

CHAPTER ELEVEN

Ladies, Converts and Demons

Men like Horsburgh and Taylor, perpetually tormented by problems of spiritual direction and evangelistic theory, men like Moule and Cassels, swamped in a slurry of administration, seem to have lost the knack of common or garden happiness – at least, it scarcely ever pops out from their writings. The refreshing affirmation that the life of a missionary in China could sometimes be sweet, liberating, exhilarating, funny, is contained mainly in the writings of 'the ladies'.

During the latter decades of the century hundreds of young women, brimming wide-open with love, trust and a burning sense of dedication, courageously uprooted themselves from pious backgrounds in Wigan or Eastbourne, Ohio or Arkansas, Swansea or Aberdeen, and went a-missioning. For the British in particular it was a neat solution to the 'surplus of marriageable women problem' caused by the disappearance, often final, of quantities of young men to the colonies; for the women themselves it offered what was usually their sole chance of a life of high endeavour and adventure overseas.

The China field had an especially high percentage of foreign women; nearly half the missionary force working in the country during the period 1885–1900 were spinsters or wives. Among them was Geraldine Guinness, an outstanding second-wave missionary of the CIM. Her family were devoted to the missionary cause; as a child she had played with Howard Taylor when he was at school in England after his escape from the Yangchow riot; later Geraldine held Bible-reading classes for the girls working in the match and bottle factories of London's East End and once, ashamed of her middle-class remoteness from their tough lives, went to live among them. Needing to test her limits further, she sailed for China as a missionary in 1888 when she was twenty-six years old and, like the Cambridge Seven, took part in a farewell dedication service in Exeter Hall. It was inspiriting enough, but what she most remembered was her parting afterwards with Andrews, her favourite street-hawker, a man with a noble heart beneath an uncouth exterior: '"I can't say no more Miss, nor I can't say what I means – but God bless you!" And tall grey-haired Andrews bent down and taking in his toil-hardened hands hers that had so often brought him blessing, he stooped and kissed them – uncouth East End hawker as he was, with as much dignity as a prince could have commanded – kissed them tenderly, reverently, silently, sobbing aloud the while.'

A gift like that for colourful narrative could not be wasted and Geraldine was encouraged by Hudson Taylor to write about her experiences from the day of her sailing – when a crowd of factory girls sang choruses of 'Crown Him, Crown Him, Crown Him' in her honour as the vessel drew away from London Docks. Once on the high seas, Geraldine and her companions set about trying to convert the other people aboard, especially the crew. This was common missionary practice and must have been regarded as an extra maritime hazard by some. But it was the only shipboard activity sanctioned by strict societies like the CIM whose regulations stated that '. . . too free intercourse with the unconverted on board unless with the distinct object of seeking their spiritual good, is to be strongly deprecated'. So the missionaries channelled their energies and there are many recorded cases of drunken boatswains, gambling cooks and wastrel deckhands who were brought to see the error of their ways during the long weeks of voyaging and who, by the time India hove in view, were joining enthusiastically in the evening singsong of Sankey's most popular hymns held on the hurricane deck.

Arriving in Shanghai, the young women were bundled to portliness in wadded Chinese gowns and sent up-country. They travelled in the local boats where they giggled over their first failures with chopsticks and loose sleeves – which would keep drooping into the fish soup – and wrote ardent letters home by the light of tattered lanterns swinging from the matted roof. Geraldine spent her first Christmas away from home in such surroundings and the exotic adventurousness of it all thrilled her, and her spirit overflowed with joy and faith. 'If, when the dear Saviour with His parting words bade us bear the message round the whole globe, did He . . . look forward and see all that obedience to His command would mean?' she wondered. 'Did he foresee our lonely Chinese junk moored on a sandy bank where deserted fishing nets dry out in the night air – Christmas Eve at midnight – Perhaps He did. At any rate, He knows now . . . I am very happy – happier now than ever I was before coming to China. Not for anything else would I be anywhere else,' she told her parents in that same Christmas letter home.

Happy cheerfulness was a valued quality among the women, who were invariably landed with the routine drudgery. Most of them could be counted upon to make the best of often dreary things. See how Geraldine and her co-workers tackled the cleaning chores all in a merry musical bustle: 'I look up from the clouds of dust where, in the outer room, I am vigorously sweeping away great heaps of rubbish, and behold Mary busy polishing windows perched on a chair out of the way of Lilian who, down on her knees, is hard at work upon the floor with hot water and flannels – no soap, no soda, but a good supply of stick-at-it and fun . . . Many a sweet hymn resounds in the rooms as we ply our tasks and the hours fly swiftly by. "I am a soldier of the Cross, a follower of the Lamb" and "All my heart I give Thee, day by day, come what may", with many another favourite.'

Their first really testing task was to learn Chinese – even though it was, Taylor once said, 'an unconverted language'. Tutors were summoned, 'untidy looking men with sun-browned faces and shaven heads under their black caps from below which hang long black pigtails; their clothes are well-padded and not over clean; their fingernails are very long and they dig them mercilessly into the books, leaving indelible marks'. Many a weary hour the nails exasperatedly dug, the anxious diligent heads bent over the multitudes of queer shapes on the page before the young worker qualified to go on itineration.

'Living in baskets' the ladies called it, for their clothes were seldom out of them as they moved around the countryside at an average of sixteen miles a day. Overland journeys were often made in 'wheelbarrows' – flat wooden carts pushed by coolies and just large enough to accommodate two people perched precariously on either side of a single wheel. It was most uncomfortable: the bang and plunge over every rock and rut, the continuous screech of un-oiled wheel, the acrid smell of coolies' sweat, the beat of sun, rain or dust-choked wind. But the ladies sang sprightly hymns as they bumped along and, Geraldine said, felt themselves 'constantly encompassed with the King's own Presence and even in the jolting wheelbarrows under the white umbrellas in the burning sun, holding sweet converse with Him by the way'.

There were other more immediate, transitory compensations: tinkle of mule-bells from a valley, azaleas blooming on a wild hillside, oxen munching among buttercups and clover, a silver pheasant with steel-blue breast strutting across their path. Receiving a friendly wave from some wayside cottage they often went inside where, amid a dim and dirty chaos of pigs and pots, straw, spinning wheels, chickens and children they would attempt to convey their message of goodwill to the busy housewife and the pipe-smoking, ancient mother-in-law.

On reaching a village they distributed preparatory leaflets about their meetings that were usually held in the early evenings when the peasants returned from the fields. When things went well, and the missionaries preached under the banyan tree or by the well to a polite attentive audience, it must have created a scene reminiscent of the innumerable sketches that appeared in the missionary magazines: 'The Prayer Meeting', 'At the Village Well', 'The Cowherd who Listened' – part of the stylised scenario of tableaux vivants which depicted in idealised visual form the highpoints of missionary endeavour. On many other occasions, not depicted in the sketches, their audience was rude, disorderly or simply non-existent; they were stoned perhaps as they left the village next day

23 The Emperor Kuang Hsu and his brother

24 A Boxer poster, found in a Manchu palace in Peking, showing a Chinese view of foreigners and their relation to China

25 Archibald and Flora Glover setting out to preach, with Hedley (*left*) and Hope in the cart, photographed just before their flight in March 1900

26 An official's retinue of men armed with bamboos to beat back crowds, and tridents to catch thieves by their clothes, largely used in 1900 for killing foreigners, as were the big knives

27 The Simcox house where five American Presbyterian missionaries and three children were burned to death on 30 June 1900

28 The British Legation barricaded with sandbags during the siege of
Peking in June and July 1900

29 Hudson Taylor (*left*), founder of the China Inland Mission, Griffith John (*centre*), of the London Missionary Society, and W. A. P. Martin (*right*), of the American Presbyterian Mission, photographed in 1905 when they had served a total of over one hundred and fifty years in China

and had to comfort themselves with the words of the ever-relevant St Paul: 'In journeyings oft, in perils of waters, in perils of robbers, in perils by the heathen, in perils among fallen brethren, in weariness and painfulness, in watchings, often in hunger and thirst . . .'

Somewhat melodramatic perhaps, but the travellers certainly did experience hardships along the way. Waterless days when they dare not ease their parched throats at the clear, cholera-ridden streams, the scalp flamed with prickly heat, and they quenched their troubles with choruses of 'We're feeding on the Living Bread, We're Drinking at the Fountain-head'. Cool dark often came before they could find shelter and they trundled along in very real perils of robbers and heathen, through shuttered villages where only scavenger dogs padded and the ragged hump of a leper lolled on a corner, one malevolent eye glittering in the moonlight. But they remained confident that, as Geraldine says, 'He had a little spot somewhere prepared just for us', and if, for that night, the spot was a filthy inn-room where bristling hogs snorted and stank in the sty next door, then it was a glorious thing to endure for His sake.

As an increasing number of dauntless young women journeyed ever further in such unguarded, insouciant fashion, the protective – and competitive – instincts of the Victorian male were fully aroused. Many missionaries pointed out that the ladies did valuable work among women and children and that they could more easily gain access to the Chinese home where they were as 'purifiers' and 'sweeteners' in a 'generally polluted' atmosphere. But other missionaries, such as the Moules, 'deprecated the unchecked development of female agency'. They felt that women were too frail and vulnerable to travel alone and they never lost their prurient fears that any young lady travelling with the sole escort of a male colleague was being exposed to the risk of a worse-than-death fate.

The secular foreign community also objected to what they called 'indiscriminate female itineration', less on account of the sexual threat posed by the missionary male which they perhaps failed to perceive, but because they felt that sooner or later one or two defenceless ladies would be assaulted or murdered which would cause an international flare-up of the kind they most wanted to avoid. They were zealous in publishing reports about the ladies' vulnerability and the bad name they were giving to foreigners in general by their unconventional behaviour. This, by a George Littledale, is typical in its anti-missionary bias, yet probably is fair in its appraisal of the Chinese reaction to the foreign women's presence. He came upon twenty-five CIM women living in a Shansi market town and wrote to the Foreign Office, 'It is hard to speak temperately of the individual or society that sends girls wholesale into the interior of such a country as China unprotected, practically uncared for and with most inadequate means . . . These poor unfortunate women, with the merest smattering of the language, are being sent about, sometimes in pairs and sometimes alone, to pray, play the guitar and sing hymns in the street, a life that none but an improper woman in China would lead, and which fosters the idea in the native mind that these girls were too bad to be allowed to remain in their own country; and they openly express the opinion that one girl must have been very bad indeed to have been sent from her own country so young . . .'

It was a sorry situation because the majority of men, Eastern and Western, insisted on regarding the female foreigners primarily as a desirable, defenceless member of the opposite sex, only secondarily as a missionary and, had they got their way, the freedom of women to work and travel would have been further curtailed. However, women who had the grit and certainty to live almost alone in the Chinese interior were not deterred by adverse comment and they seemed generally unperturbed by the anxious masculine speculation on their behalf.

However, the anxiety was not entirely misplaced, for some missionaries encouraged their converts in practices that seemed specifically designed to arouse violent hostility among the people. Among the Protestant societies, the CIM pursued the most actively aggressive policy against the native religions: as many Buddhists were vegetarians, they encouraged their converts to eat meat publicly and openly, for instance. They also took a gruesomely fervent pleasure in arranging the ceremonial destruction of Buddhist images and ancestral tablets. In the *China's Millions Annual* for 1889, missionary Emily Whitchurch records her high success rate in this esoteric field. 'April 22nd. Had the joy of smashing and burning the idols in two homes. April 24th. Went to the east suburb to remove idols. April 26th. Went to Wang-tung 15 *li* away with a man from the Refuge to see him take down his idols. (My fourth visit to the place for the same glorious purpose.) As we entered the village a man met us who asked, "Have you come to smash idols?" I had quite a hearty welcome and the yard was fairly filled while Mr Lo and I talked to the people. Then my convert brought out his idols and burnt them . . .'

Naturally enough crowds would gather to watch the spectacle of the foreign woman in her strange garb raising hallelujahs of joy as the flames blistered the gilt and plaster, blackened the blank eyes of the little home-made buddhas, and they would gather too to see missionaries arriving armed with posters, guitars, decorated texts and even magic lanterns to illustrate the Visit of the Magi or the Story of the Ten Virgins. Such unusual events were enough to keep the converts, indeed the whole placid neighbourhood, agog for weeks. But when the missionaries moved on, leaving the 'infant Church' to support itself under the guidance of a native pastor, there followed an inevitable cooling off of ardour that was often irreversible.

Missionary conferences returned again and again to this theme: 'Deepening the spiritual life of our converts', or 'Arousing the women from their state of intellectual torpor' or, basically, 'How to combat backsliding'. 'What is needed,' thundered one missionary delegate, 'to rouse the people from their state of spiritual coma is a galvanic shock.' And he continued, carried away by the daring modernity of his own image, 'We are the battery. Along our helpless lips may flow the swift electric current of His Word, quickening the dead into perfect life. Ours to keep the battery in perfect order, the box open and the current flowing.' For in China the missionaries so often felt that the current was a mere trickle that ran but shallowly across what one termed 'the vast gulf between the greatness of revelation and the meagreness of its reception, between the almost incredible wealth of apostolic thought and the poverty of the convert's faith'.

Certainly it was true that the proportion of backsliders in China was dishearteningly high, and one major reason was the missionaries' pre-occupation with the rules of Victorian morality. They forbade their church members to watch any form of dramatic entertainment for instance – in a country where travelling theatres and operas were the most popular and widespread form of entertainment. They forbade them to indulge in any form of gambling – in a country where every sweet vendor had a little gambling wheel that offered a toddler a 'double or quits' chance for his single piece of cash.

In addition, converts were subject to a variety of social and economic pressures that can be illustrated by reference to the many backsliding case-histories on record. There was Pastor Lin Sing who, it transpired, had joined the Protestant Church because he needed foreign allies in his long-standing feud against his neighbours, who had the local Catholic priest on their side; little 'Peach Petal' who faithfully determined to become a Bible woman until the 'heathen' son of a rich official was betrothed to her; Mao Fi-pi, the beancurd-maker's assistant, who conscientiously refused to buy oil for the altar in his employer's shop, until he was threatened with the sack; and Lo T'ang, the shoemaker's assistant, who was faced with the same ultimatum when he refused to work on Sundays; merchant O Kwang who prayed for God's guidance over how to increase his capital, and left the church when the tea-junk he had invested in foundered on a sand-bank; and catechist Matthew Tai who left the CMS for the American Presbyterians because the latter paid more liberal travelling expenses. ('Matthew' would have been the name given to the catechist on his Christian baptism. There were many Paul Wongs, Luke Li-pis, and newly-dubbed Eunices, Lydias and Marthas among the Bible women. It was a form of naming magic that appealed to the Chinese.)

But the naming itself was not sufficient bond and the experience of many missionaries was pit-holed with the disillusionments and failures of backsliding. Sometimes their reserves of loving-kindness, charity and tolerance were eroded quite away, leaving them full of hatred and contempt for the people they worked among. Wherever missionaries gathered it was commonplace for them to condemn the Chinese as a 'covetous', 'licentious', 'dishonest', 'materialistic' people, encrusted with 'superstition, ignorance and sin'. Worst of all, they remained in a state of complacent unawareness about the true meaning of 'sin'. When a Chinaman complained that his sins were heavy he usually meant that his worldly troubles were very great. It was an equation that came naturally to those imbued with the temporal morality of Confucianism, but it horrified the guilt-ridden Protestant missionaries, especially when compounded by the error of expecting any Christian confession of 'sin' to be at once rewarded with a trouble-free life.

So few converts truly understood the concepts of sin and repentance in the mystical Christian sense that those who did show evidence of real understanding and deep spiritual conviction were given every encouragement to take up the vocation of spreading the Gospel. Promising young men were offered training courses at the theological colleges established in the treaty ports and those who qualified were then ordained as pastors or ministers. This meant a considerable rise in social status for many, because the Chinese were ever ready to respect the acquisition of learning, however and wherever it had been obtained. It was sometimes difficult therefore to distinguish the truly dedicated pastor from the status-seeker who was, as one missionary put it, 'content merely to don the sky-blue scholar's robe, adjust his goggles and, with the affected gait of the literati, ascend the platform and discourse'.

However, there certainly were a number of totally dedicated Chinese Christians enrolled in the Church; one of them, the first to ever rate a full-scale biography in English, was Pastor Hsi. The biography was written by Mrs Howard Taylor, that is, the former Geraldine Guinness who married her childhood playmate, Hudson's son Howard, in China. Her hero, Hsi, was a Confucian scholar who had been a heavy opium smoker until he was cured in a mission refuge. The experience filled him with the passionate zeal

of the 'hard case convert' and he gave the rest of his life unstint-
ingly to the Christian cause. He sold his family heirlooms to open
his own refuge, with the words 'Heavenly Invitation Office'
inscribed in gilt above the door. Addicts could stay for long-term
cures and Hsi supplied them with his own make of opium pills
which came in three optimistic varieties: Life Imparting, Life
Establishing, Health Restoring. Their reputation for success was
so great that some of his church members concocted cheap imita-
tions of them to sell in a shop opposite the refuge – which caused
a serious rift in Hsi's 'pastorate'.

Hsi had another skill that he used in the service of his faith – he
could cure those afflicted with 'demon possession'. At least, he
firmly believed he could. He chose the words 'Demon Overcomer' as his baptismal name and engaged in a life-long, very
personal battle against Satan and his cohorts. Hsi's belief in his
own miraculous powers was shared by other members of the CIM,
as Geraldine Taylor makes clear in her account of them: 'Hsi laid
his hands on the woman and in the name of Jesus commanded the
evil spirits to leave her and return no more. From that moment
the trouble ceased, Mrs Chang became quiet and self-possessed.
All the symptoms of her strange disorder passed away and she
was soon as earnest as her husband in seeking to bring others to
the Saviour.' That was written in 1903, by which time, as Geraldine admits, there was a 'tendency in some quarters to doubt the
very existence of a personal devil, a malignant spirit of evil with
hosts of emissaries to work his will. This perhaps is hardly to be
wondered at in Christian countries where the power of Satan is
restricted and it is clearly inexpedient for him to appear in his
true colours . . . In heathendom his tactics are open and his aims
apparent.'

In support of her thesis, Geraldine could have pointed out that
missionaries who lived for years among the superstitious Chinese
were the most likely to share their belief in the existence of intan-
gible evil presences. The most prominent explorer of this shadowy
field was Dr Livingston Nevius, an American Presbyterian
missionary and expert on both 'angelology' and 'satanology'.
When writing his exhaustive book, *Demon Possession*, Nevius

sent a circular to all his Protestant colleagues asking for any personal evidence they could offer on the subject. The response was very large, for missionaries and pastors were often called upon to 'flush out the demons' when native remedies failed. The possessed manifested a variety of alarming symptoms, supposedly in imitation of the particular spirit that had control over them. They flailed their limbs and leaped about, twittered like birds, crawled like snakes, shouted like soldiers or snorted like hogs, they rolled on the floor with mirth or threw knives at anyone in sight. The Christian treatment was to read relevant parts of the New Testament and pray over the victims, and the result, according to Nevius, was frequently successful. 'One feels oneself transported back to the Apostles and is compelled to believe that the dominion of Satan is by no means broken yet,' he concludes, after a moving account of a particularly efficacious 'laying on of hands' during which a demon-possessed housewife was converted to a devout Bible woman.

Nevius' book indeed transports one to a medieval if not a positively apostolic world and by the time of its appearance in 1895 a number of his younger colleagues in the field were somewhat uneasy about it, for intellectual reasons which a reviewer in the *American Journal of Medical Sciences* made brutally plain. 'Dr Nevius, instead of converting the heathen, was perverted by them. Such a book would be impossible for any man who had not himself been far removed for a long time from the best civilising influences . . . When Christian-educated ministers take the lead in such a demoralising witches' Sabbath as is depicted in this book, then does the gap between orthodox theology and pure science seem wide indeed . . .'

But Nevius belonged to that older generation of missionaries who, seeing themselves as the first brave prophets of truth in benighted primitive heathendom, had created an apostolic context for themselves in China. The props, common to any Eastern agrarian economy from Palestine to Manchuria, were there in abundance: wells, water jars, ploughs; bereft widows, ragged lepers, sowing peasants, oppressive officials; wily 'heathen' priests idling in golden temples – and ordinary people beset with demons from the nether world. To the Bible-saturated missionary mind all this brought a sense of familiarity, security and meaningfulness; it was part of the romance and adventure of the evangelistic life and a constant source of imagery and parable for their sermons and writings.

The theme is recurrent; few pressed the parallels further than J. Campbell Gibson in the introduction to his book about missionary methods: 'In the missionary field, especially perhaps in China, the world of eighteen hundred years ago springs again into life and reality ... The Chinese Dragon takes the place of the Roman Eagle, consuls, pro-consuls, praetors, deputies move across the scene in the persons of Chinese mandarins ... The Indifferent Gallio ... Demetrius, crafty maker of shrines and Alexander the provoking copper-smith are our next door neighbours ... Stoic philosophers encounter us once more in the market place, muttering the question, "What would these babblers say?" and dismiss us with their polite but chilling formula, "We will hear thee again of this matter." Some cleave to us ... the woman named Damaris is a familiar figure and the photograph of the beloved Persis with her bound feet and her quaint old walking staff and her Chinese Bible, hangs on my study wall and is a daily stimulant to patient and faithful work ...' In fact, Gibson concludes, 'the book of the Apostles is for us not so much a record of the past as a picture of the present and a handbook for daily use ...'

Once this premise had been accepted it provided a familiar backdrop for action on otherwise unfamiliar terrain and also scope for creation of colourful *idola* and roles for the missionaries, who felt themselves in a direct line of descent from the heroes of the New Testament. Gibson modestly disclaims: 'The places of Saint Paul and Saint Peter, of Timothy and Titus are but poorly filled by the modern missionary ...', but not too poorly perhaps. This picturesque dramaturgy was lost upon most of the converts because much of it was alien and bewildering, but it made a great impact on a few who accepted it with such wholeheartedness that they often failed to distinguish its metaphor from reality.

Pastor Hsi was one of these and he never lost his zest for the divinely inspired apostle role. He itinerated tirelessly on a cart that had the words 'Holy Religion of Jesus' emblazoned in red characters on its outside and his clothing bore the motto, 'Jesus came into the world to save sinners'. If any missionary had the temerity to query any of his methods, his reply was always the same and always unanswerable: 'If it were a question of my own wishes, I should never have done this, but if the Lord desires to do this work through me, can I refuse?'

Overt criticisms of Hsi and his work were, in any case, an embarrassment and tended to remain unvoiced when, after a few years, Hsi settled in Shansi to establish his own mission station, with opium refuge, school and dispensary. 'Middle Eden' Hsi called it, and it became something of a showpiece for the CIM, a truly Christian community supported and organised entirely by the Chinese themselves. Converts came for miles on Sundays to listen to Hsi's spirited sermons, sing hymns, then gather in the courtyards under the shade of the old vines to share the meals of rice and vegetables they had brought. Some elected to stay there permanently and submit themselves to Hsi's strict regimen of rules and duties. Brother Ti-teh, for instance, whose tasks were to look after the sheep, 'to supply water and salt, praying to God to keep the beasts in health', while Brother Li Chang had to attend to the stables, the cow byre, the farm gate, 'also to sweep around and in his leisure to study the Scriptures'. Gentle Princess (one of Hsi's numerous nieces) had to sweep three rooms before breakfast, spin thread after it, study, and feed the chickens after dinner – and 'wait until the hen has left the nest to pick up the eggs'. If she defaulted, 'her old Aunt with a small stick is to beat her five times on the hand'. No one living in Middle Eden was permitted to attend fairs or theatricals or smoke a pipe (neither dry nor water) or drink wine or gossip in doorways or sleep in the day-time – save during the harvest of the fourth moon when the work was particularly strenuous.

Thus Pastor Hsi, overcomer of demons, created round himself the very pattern of the stern devout Victorian household. He was the proud and pious paterfamilias and his establishment offered security and support to all those who obeyed its rules. Nowadays one might find those rules aptly illustrative of a process that one historian describes as the erection of 'many little foibles of the European Reformed Churches into dogmas of the Christian religion' and their subsequent importation into irrelevant 'heathen' circumstances. But missionaries like Geraldine Taylor did not see it like that. She loved to visit the place, to watch the purposeful, orderly comings and goings of catechists, dispensary assistants, quaint little nieces with their eggs or spun thread, and, later, to join in the evening services when Pastor Hsi, his white hair and beard aglow in the moonlight, led them all in such lovely hymns of thanksgiving as 'Bringing in the Sheaves'. Middle Eden it did indeed seem to her on such occasions, a meaningful, thriving Christian community set in the middle of heathen Shansi like a beacon light; but to others Middle Eden was an incongruous parody, an obstinate irrelevance sticking out of provincial China like a sore thumb.

CHAPTER TWELVE

Some Time in Shanghai

In the year 1890 a total of 1,296 Protestant missionaries were working in China; more than half of them were British; 589 of them were men; they claimed to have 37,287 faithful Chinese communicants; in May, 446 of them gathered in Shanghai to attend the biggest missionary conference ever held in the country.

Shanghai was a convenient and appropriate location, a great trading centre with an estimated native and foreign population of two hundred thousand, the place where Westernisation was most in the ascendant. Those desolate stretches of marsh which the first group of CIM missionaries had seen as they limped into Woosung Creek twenty-four years before on the tattered *Lammermuir* now sagged queasily under an ever-growing burden of bricks, macadam, iron, cement and steel. There was a clatter of cotton and paper mills, silk filatures, dock and building yards, gas and water works, godowns, wharves and factories that pumped filthy smoke into the air, filthy waste into the sea and, into every ear, the continual clang and chuff of machinery in relentless motion. The busy harbour was alert with red and white striped lighthouses containing keepers of the first, second and third class, and called the West Saddle, the East Volcano and the Gutzlaff – the last named after that pioneer Pomeranian missionary, perhaps because of his 'intolerable assumption of omniscience'. For always the missionaries thought comfortably of God when they saw the lighthouse beacons flashing over the dark ocean wastes, sending firm, kind warning signals to all approaching vessels about the hidden hazards of rock and tide when the fogs lay low along the shore, as they often did.

To some of the young men fresh out from Europe and America in search of adventure, Shanghai had become unhazardous and secure to the point of boredom. 'Where o' where is the mysterious East we came to see?' asked a bachelor contributor to an 1890 number of *The Shanghai Rattle*. 'All I find here is debility and debts, mugginess, mosquitoes and moonlight music, punkahs, perspiration and interminable parties.' They were going to open a Co-op next, he said, and he might as well be back in Rochdale, Lancashire.

Nevertheless, newly-arrived young whites ('griffins' as they were called) knew they had never had it so good. 'We had a ravenous appetite for exercise,' wrote one of them, C. M. Dyce, in a swamp of nostalgia for his youthful days in 'The Model Settlement'. Fives, rackets, cricket, rowing were essential activities for 'shaking up the old liver' after the previous night's 'beer, balls and brandy' – as it was put by one of the many local humorists who relied heavily on alliteration for their laughs. 'It is in my opinion impossible for a young man to have too much of the manly sports,' Dyce concluded, and with some justification, for his liver survived the life for thirty years – a survival that he attributed partly to the fact that he never once over-heated his brain with the 'intricate and quaint phraseology' of the Chinese language.

There was no need, for one had but to shout 'bring-come' and everything would arrive. First the water-carrier to fill the cool green-glaze Ningpo tub for the daily bath, then the 'number-two boy' with the glass of 'breakfast claret', the steak and eggs (both so cheap one couldn't afford not to eat them), and then the same shout would summon the jinrikisha coolie who pulled one to the office for the business of the day. Most griffins were in silk or in tea, a few in the small 'muck and truck' firms that exported buffalo horns and hides, lampwick grass, horsehair, melon seeds, Mongolian wool, nutgalls, donkey skins, dried lily flowers and rush hats. The silk men were superior, elevated above the coarse rattle of hats and even tea by the beauty of their merchandise.

'Chinese silks are the best in the world,' Dyce wrote defiantly, 'and none of them nobler than classical Tsatlee . . . It is of the purest white colour and has a lustre which is seen in no other silk; it possesses a quality of such nervous strength that it almost seems alive in your hands.'

But most of Dyce's youthful enthusiasms took wing after four o' clock when the hongs closed and he and his chums strolled over to the Horse Bazaar to look at the ponies – which were also called 'griffins', perhaps because they were somewhat swollen-headed and coltish creatures, like the young men watching them. It was promenade time along the Bund for the shipping agents and lawyers in their phaetons, the tea-bosses (called 'Chasees') and the bank clerks, the brokers of bills, shares, insurance, coal, freight and metal who had driven about 'all day long in little basket carriages and lived active, merry lives with little responsibility', in Dyce's opinion. The predominantly commercial scene was, of course, 'much enlivened by the presence' of the ladies who, fortunately, settled in Shanghai during the 80s in greater numbers and so helped 'to counteract the demoralising influences which are inseparable from association with inferior races and absence of home ties'.

The ladies too led lives of little responsibility as they circulated in carriages to distribute shoals of calling-cards, arrange the next day's tiffin, gossip about the rising price of oysters and pheasants, the daring décolletage worn twice by the wife of the Austrian Legation Secretary, the amorous reputation of the globetrotting millionaire just bowled in from San Francisco. Some of the ladies were undoubtedly merry as well as irresponsible, but they usually looked washed out and slightly breathless during the hot days in their tight dresses, their pallid cheeks lacking the glow imparted by indulgence in any of the 'manly sports'. For they were at their best in the evening, when the sun's bite loosened and they girded themselves for entertainment – the latest of the Shanghai Amateur Dramatic Society perhaps, a band concert in the park or just the eating of dinners which must have been occupation enough, beginning, as they did, about seven o'clock with sherry, then on to soup, fish, entrées, an extra joint, and on again to curries, cheeses, salads, followed by sweets, desserts, fruits, and all helped down with libations of wine and port.

The lustreless, stiff-necked figure of the missionary was very much on the fringe of this cosmopolitan and hectic round. By this time considerable mutual antagonism existed between the mercantile and missionary communities and there were few echoes of the individualistic early days when, for example, the mercantile firm of Jardine Matheson helped to finance missionary James Legge's translations of the Chinese classics. Now, most secular foreigners who had stamina to write at book length about their experiences in China included a chapter that was critical, and/or derisive of missionary endeavour. Harshly typical of the genre was *English Life in China* by one Major Knollys, which aroused the fury of the mission press when it appeared. Knollys charged missionaries with 'the performance of perfunctory duties in a perfunctory fashion' and the pursuit of both 'luxurious appurtenances' and 'a social status to which their birth and breeding by no means entitle them'. The missionary, said Knollys, 'lives in a perpetual state of bicker with the rest of the foreign community' mainly because of his unflagging quest for money, 'for which he appeals with a mixture of petulance and the air of a man denied his sacred rights'.

Missionaries who had lived for years in the treaty ports were familiar with such barbs, though they could not ignore them. At the 1890 Shanghai Conference Arthur Moule bitterly lamented the numbers of foreign residents who regarded the missionaries as outsiders and who refused the duty that was 'obligatory not optional to come out actively on the missionary side in the great fight'. He urged the delegates to claim their 'right to the guiding relationship' and assured them that this was what many wayward Westerners secretly wanted. It was a speech with just that mixture of arrogance, irascibility and self-righteousness about which Knollys complained and it typified the attitude of many older missionaries in China who had watched the generally influential advance of Western trade and industrialisation and who knew that, by comparison and in spite of years of effort, their impact on the moral and spiritual life of the nation was minimal.

Yet if they were not to be the vanguard, most of the conference delegates still longed to ride high in the wake of industrial progress and their confident, even strident tone perfectly reflected the prevailing attitude of political, social and economic assertiveness which the major Western powers, and Japan, had begun to adopt towards China. 'Through the transparent robes of missionary humility,' remarked one contemporary commentator astutely, 'may generally be traced the spirit of imperialism impatient of opposition and delay.' It was a spirit never more manifest than in a speech delivered by an American Presbyterian on the conference's opening day. 'The conquest of this country in 1860,' he began, 'may be likened to the conquest of primeval America. It gave us access; but, as in the one case, a luxuriant wild growth of centuries cumbered the earth and must be removed before the settlers could find a home and congenial surroundings, so here were found similar conditions of a moral character, the elimination of which was necessary to the introduction of that higher civilisation that is so indispensable to the best welfare of mankind.'

Only a few voices demurred from the thesis that the immoral swamps of the Chinese character had to be cleansed and tamed; the differences that arose were rather over methods of approach. What indigenous offshoots should the stern civilisers permit the Chinese to retain? What graftings should be attempted? What areas should be totally laid bare to prepare the way for the reception of the unsullied Word? Such questions were raised on several fronts; one of them was the heated division of opinion about the Word's actual presentation.

The Word, all agreed, was the Bible, but some delegates wanted the Bible Societies to provide interpretative commentaries and notes that would forge helpful links between its wisdom and that of the Chinese classics. In some places, they pointed out, the Bible was so misinterpreted that it was banned as a politically seditious book (to what extent this *was* a misrepresentation was not discussed); anyway, the British Foreign Office had warned missionaries against distributing it without any explanatory comments. Other delegates however felt it was tantamount to

145

heresy to even suggest that the Word of God could not be compre-
hended by any living creature 'unless it were accompanied by
notes of man's production'. 'We must give them the sincere milk
of the Word,' thundered the senior representative of the British
and Foreign Bible Society, 'and its spirit will work in them.' And
he told them not to forget the revered John Wycliffe who had
presented his Bible without annotation to the rough ploughboys
of old England, and had *they* not understood it? (Anyone sufficiently in touch with parallel controversies at home could have
riposted that recent researches in biblical history had given rise to
widespread doubts about literal interpretations, and that not only
inspired ploughboys but many a country parson reached for the
latest commentary before committing himself to the pulpit.)

The issue that brought into sharpest focus the differences
between those who favoured a policy of grafting, adapting,
compromising, and those intent on total 'cleansing' in order to
're-build' was that of ancestor-worship. A forward-looking note
in this recurrent debate was struck by W. A. P. Martin, still head
of Peking's T'ung-wen Kuan, who made a courageous and
impassioned 'Plea for the Toleration of Ancestor Worship'. He
argued that, instead of pitting themselves against an ancient
tradition which had so much native reverence and benevolence
in it, which was indeed 'the very keystone of the Chinese social
system', missionaries should think in terms of a modified and 'un-
Europeanised' form of Christianity. They should be content to
'prune off the idolatrous excesses' (which he defined as the ascrip-
tion of divine attributes to the souls of the dead) and leave the reformation of the system 'to the influence of the Divine Truth when
it gets a firmer hold on the native mind'. But Martin's reasoning
was highly contentious, for it was indissolubly linked in many
minds with the compromises and casuistries of the Roman Catholics who had always envisaged the Christianisation of China as a
long process of cultural adaptation and spiritual transformation,
not as the hacking-down and clearing-away operation that
appealed to energetic Protestants bred in the pioneer tradition.

Moreover, and worse yet, ancestor worship was the central
tenet of Confucianism, the official, indigenous cult which the

missionaries found most confusing. In the main, they preferred to rally their forces against the obvious arch-enemies of Taoism and Buddhism, which were decently equipped with rituals, dogmas and a variety of minor deities. Confucianism was fluid and informal by comparison, lacking an established priesthood, a distinctive organisation or any hard and fast doctrine about the relationship of body and spirit. It was hardly a religion at all in the Western sense, but it was socially all-pervasive none the less, and possessed of an unnerving ethic which sometimes seemed so akin to Christian morality that the unwary could be tempted to form allegiance with it. Confucius, after all, also extolled the virtues of philanthropy, frugality, understanding and love. 'With coarse rice for my food, with water for my drink and my bended arm for my pillow, I have joy still present with me,' said Confucius. 'Love it is,' said Confucius, 'that makes a neighbourhood beautiful. Love is of more importance to people than fire and water. I have seen men die by walking in fire and water, but I have never seen men die through walking in love . . . Learning is the product of thought, and thinking is like digging a deep well. One gets only muddy water at first but, when down deep enough, one finds the clear water of understanding.'

A considerable number of the Chinese literati, drilled from childhood in Confucianism's cool and careful ethic, were cultured, dignified men, as the missionaries had to admit. They were as humane and practical as the circumstances allowed in their dealings with others, and as obedient, austere, conservative and rational within their own social context as any Puritan in his. But their very subtlety and sophistication posed special threats, for, as one conference delegate explained, 'If Western philosophy and science comes to China divorced from Christianity, Confucian scholars will accept the new learning with proud self-complacency and will find in it only a confirmation and more elaborate illustration of the past teachings of Confucian scholars for at least the last two thousand years.' So there was a shrewdness there, a wiliness that was 'of the earth, earthy and so exactly suited to the commonplace matter-of-fact-ness of the Chinese mind'. For, in the last analysis, the Confucianist, however intelligent and moral he was, lacked that tense yearning for the eternal, that consciousness of the mystery and the fire, that ultimate knowledge of spiritual grace which was granted to the Christian.

The missionaries in Shanghai, seeking renewal of the tension and the fire, were warmed by the sense of dedicated, relatively unified purpose that the conference evoked and by the old-fashioned firebrand oratory of the venerable 'greats' in the China field, such as Dr Nevius and Hudson Taylor. They hammered again their own obsessive themes. Nevius, authority on demon-worship, urged his audience to remind the natives frequently 'of the constantly recurring calamities of flood and famine' that were sent to teach them dependence on the All-Powerful Ruler rather than on their own 'fickle, undiscriminating spirits of catastrophe'. Taylor was still counting the same untouched heads in his eternal arithmetic of damnation and salvation. 'If there are 250,000,000 people in China, some 50,000,000 families, and if we had 1,000 evangelists and colporteurs reaching fifty families a day, in 1,000 days, or less than three years, an offer of the Gospel or a verbal message might be given to all . . .'

Taylor was ageing now, his eyes dimming 'in China's service'; but he and his outstanding contemporaries were still men of indomitable presence, very capable of imposing their strong wills on the gathering. Thus, although voices of dissent were heard – pleading for an extension of non-sectarian, humanitarian institutions, for a broadening of educational curricula, for a general leavening of Old Testament severity with the new cultural tolerance – they did not carry the majority with them. After Martin's plea for the toleration of ancestor worship, it was Hudson Taylor who rose to repudiate it in the most scathing and uncompromising way. He concluded his challenge with the request that all those who agreed with him and disagreed with Martin should stand up and be counted. Nearly everyone in the hall stood up; the idol-burners were still in the ascendant. 'It is the narrow way that leads to the heavenly country,' one of those who gladly stood up reminded the few who did not. 'The Lord Himself made it narrow and we cannot make it broad.'

After a marathon twelve days of talking and with this as one of their last conclusions, the delegates dispersed. Earnest, sober men and women thrust away from their own kind into the bustle of the Shanghai streets, where the languid ladies and merry brokers bowling past in their carriages, the heedless, natty bachelors hurrying towards the Horse Bazaar, were a forceful reminder that it was not only the innumerable Chinese who needed direction to the narrow way. For, when all the hymns and speeches were over and the missionaries returned to their stations and itinerations, the way remained a lonely and stony one for many. It was to become stonier yet in the next decade, leading some to agony and glory through the bloodiest gateway of all.

PART FOUR

Give me any person . . . a martyr, if you wish . . . a
saint . . . He'll take what he gets for . . . what he wishes
it to be. Ah, it is what I have always wanted, he'll say,
looking terror and betrayal straight in the eye. Why
not: face the inevitable and call it what you have always
wanted. How to come out on top, going under.

Edward Albee, TINY ALICE

CHAPTER THIRTEEN

Hellfire and Hankow

The prevailing tone of the 1890 conference was optimistic and self-congratulatory – more missionaries in China than ever before, more mission schools and hospitals, more converts and places of worship – but several warning notes were sounded. The most fateful of these, as things turned out, came from the speaker who described the variety of secret societies which, for centuries, had honeycombed the Chinese social fabric. Some had worthy social purposes (the protection of aged widows, the prevention of opium-smoking), others were simply quaint (for the burning of specially fragrant Tibetan incense, for the nurture of baby birds that had fallen from their nests), but, as the speaker pointed out, a large number of them had always been political, sometimes subversive.

There was the Eight Trigrams Sect, for example, which took its name from the Book of Changes and symbolised the division of the universe into eight 'mansions'; the White Lily Sect, considered by the authorities to be the most dangerous of all, with a long history of sedition and riot dating back to the twelfth century; and the I Ho Chuan, the Righteous Harmony Fists, a complex offshoot of the other two, whose adherents first made a nuisance of themselves in 1727 when they were accused of stirring up the people by practising their cult of self-defensive boxing. The aims of these politically disruptive societies were varied and changeable: to overthrow the Manchu dynasty, to oust all foreigners from the country or cunningly to achieve both by the instigation of attacks on foreigners designed to bring the Manchus into open conflict with the West – a situation that would probably result in the dynasty's collapse.

In 1890 however these rebellious elements among the people still seemed under control; of more immediate concern to foreign interests was the growth of xenophobia within government circles. This was fostered by a conservative faction which felt that China was being mercilessly exploited and weakened by the intrusion of Western trade, ideas and institutions; from its members, it was suspected, emanated the fresh burst of anti-Christian propaganda which appeared in a collection of documents on state questions published during the late 1880s.

One of the first foreigners to draw Western attention to these was Timothy Richard who had recently severed his connection with the Baptist Missionary Society to become editor of the *Shih Pao* (*The Times*), a newspaper published in Tientsin. A strange move for him to make, on the face of it, but the paper was one of the only six Chinese newspapers in the Empire and the only one, except for the official *Peking Gazette*, that circulated freely in the northern provinces. Richard used his new post to disseminate his liberal and imaginative views among the educated as he had always hoped to do. He published articles and charts to show how telegraph and railway systems could improve communications in China and wrote at somewhat fulsome length in praise of all the clever go-ahead schemes the Japanese were busy implementing that would soon take them into the international top league. Richard's unusual position also gave him insight into the general mood of China and his assessment of it was, as he told the delegates of the 1890 conference, that the missionary body was 'standing on a volcano' which was likely to erupt into violent persecution unless urgent steps were taken to prevent it.

Richard was correct, but he had the habit of being wise before his time, and little attention was paid to his gloomy prophecies until the next year, when a series of riots broke out in the River Yangtze area. The Great Long River, Girdle of China, had been dominated by British trading interests since it was partly opened to the West in 1860 and British missionaries had been among the first to seize the opportunity of settling in its treaty ports. The very first had been Griffith John, the hopeful young Welshman who, with Joseph Edkins, had tried to win the confidence of the Taiping leaders in the late 1850s.

In 1861 John had reached the treaty port of Hankow, a great inland trading centre for eight provinces, including its own fertile, densely populated Hupeh. John took to it at once: 'I have not seen a place that I like better in every respect than this,' he told the Secretary of the London Missionary Society in an early letter. 'There is a vastness about it that takes my fancy wonderfully. The Chinese have well called it the middle or the heart of the Empire. From here missionaries can penetrate the country in every direction.' As William Cassels found his chosen piece of heathendom in Paoning, so John stuck to this wealthy, fever-ridden city where two rivers met on a muddy plain; in mission circles he soon became known as 'John of Hankow'; he stayed there, with but slight interruption, for forty-five years.

The milestones of his missionary life were fairly predictable: the first seedy rented quarters in a back-alley and the first chapel in a disused ancestral hall. A thoroughgoing Welshman, John's powers of oratory were great, the fountainhead of his own spiritual sustenance, and he never tired of expressing his conviction that 'the living voice was the most effective instrument for spreading the Gospel message'. He preached indoors and out, morning, noon and night, year in, year out, 'wearing them down' as he put it, 'with the glorious persistence of the Word'. He travelled in wide 'circuits of itineration' that took him back again and again to the same street corner or market square until he became a familiar, if still quaint, figure on many a local landscape – the short, muscular body, the black springy beard, keen flashing eyes and, above all, that impassioned and resonant voice. 'Grace, grit and gumption' he once said were the essential missionary qualities; these he felt he possessed. His views were outspoken and uncompromising and it was he who, speaking at the first Protestant Conference held in Shanghai in 1877, expressed the extreme evangelistic position which was frequently quoted by those who attacked the blinkered inflexibility of the missionary approach.

'We are not here to develop the resources of the country, not for the advancement of commerce, not for the mass promotion of civilisation,' John thundered, 'but to do battle with the powers of darkness, to save men from sin and conquer China for Christ.'

For the first ten years of his life in Hankow, John and his colleagues were the only missionaries in permanent residence, but by no means the only foreigners. Traders of many nations had early appreciated its strategic commercial position and an extensive foreign settlement grew up along the river bank outside the walls of the teeming native city. Traffic along the Yangtze thickened to include everything from Western gunboats and passenger steamers to flimsy bumboats selling armfuls of fresh Chinese cabbage for a single *cash*. The Chinese tea trade was still flourishing and the queenly tea-clippers raced each other home from the Hankow Bund, the record being set in 1877 when the *London Castle* left Hankow at 1 am on 24th May, made Port Said on 22nd June and hove in sight of the Sussex Downs at 7 pm on 2nd July. Back in Hankow, lighthouses swathed the dark river from Ruined Fort Point and Bouncer Island; the foreign-run Customs Office was in constant uproar and French, Italians, British and Americans all pursued the mysterious and leisurely-sounding occupation of 'tide-waiting'. The advent of so much frank and aggressive money-making and industrialisation had a deleterious effect upon the local citizenry, according to John. He often lamented their cupidity and wrote that '. . . two or three hundred *cash* a week have a greater attraction for the average Chinaman than the salvation of his soul'.

At any rate, increased prosperity attracted more of those concerned with soul saving and, during the relatively calm decade of the 1880s, a number of other missionary societies followed in the wake of trade and began work in Hankow. The CIM were next there, then the American Presbyterians, the Spanish Order of St Augustine, the Canadian Baptists, the Quakers, the Danish Mission and the American Board of Missions. The *Times* correspondent George Morrison noted that, as a result, Hankow was a happy hunting-ground for rice Christians who, 'with timely lapses of grace are said to succeed in being converted in turn by all the missions from the Augustines to the Quakers'. Most of the missionaries resided within the foreign settlement which evoked another of Morrison's pleasantly sardonic comments to the effect that 'every visitor to Hankow . . . who is a supporter of missionary effort is pleased to find that his preconceived notions of the hardness and discomforts of the missionary lot in China are entirely false . . . Among the most comfortable residences in the port are the quarters of the missionaries. . .'

John's mission expanded rapidly to include a 'comfortable residence' for his family, several chapels, a hospital and leper asylum, a boys' school and a Hankow Tract Society depot for the printing and distribution of books and tracts. Some 340,000 of them were circulated in the year 1883 alone; they bore such titles as 'The Need for Repentance', 'The Forgiveness of Sin Plan', 'The Gate of Wisdom and Virtue'. John's favourite element was his large brick Gospel Meeting Hall where he preached to six-hundred-strong gatherings that were segregated by sex on opposite sides of the main aisle in conformity with Chinese etiquette.

An admiring colleague once described a typical Sunday service in the Hall thus: 'There is a distinct smell of Chinaman and Chinaman's clothes, although Boyle's ventilators are groaning in the roof and many windows are open. Among the congregation are many aged men and women, old pilgrims to Zion who will soon see the King in His beauty. There are bright boys with hymn books and Bibles tied up in their handkerchiefs looking very important; girls with gay attire, hair tightly braided and all expectant. The inevitable babies with their doting mothers who have several ways of keeping them quiet, such as pinching their legs, compressing their windpipes etc., all quite orthodox to the Chinese, although sufficiently horrifying to the lady missionaries who are keeping the female crowd in order.' Then Griffith John appears, wearing the black Inverness cloak that he uses to great rhetorical effect as he paces to and fro in the fire of his earnestness. His impassioned intensity reveals 'his knowledge of the people's trials, persecutions and stumbling-blocks and a starting tear here and there shows that his beautiful resonant voice has carried a comforting softening message to the heart. Then comes a change.

He dwells on sin and its character in the sight of God. How keen is his analysis of the Chinaman's self-deception; how scathing the exposure of duplicity, falsehood and cunning; how terrible the picture of the wreck and ruin which are the wages of sin . . .'

Hellfire, to which unrepentant sinners were indubitably consigned, was a real and vital part of John's cosmography. But he found it difficult to resolve the contradiction inherent in that belief as to what would be the destiny of heathens who had never heard of the Christian God. Obviously, this question had for long been a missionary pre-occupation and, by the 1880s, the Protestant societies were split into liberal and traditional factions on the issue. The eternal damning of the ignorant to hell simply on account of their ignorance became an increasingly unpopular and untenable position; in one modern historian's view, 'eternal punishment received literally no attention in missionary literature after the turn of the century'. But Griffith John was a thoroughly nineteenth-century man and his solution of the difficulty was an unconsciously comic blend of exclusive Calvinism and conscientious humanitarianism, which, in his addresses given to missionaries in America, he was wont to elucidate thus: 'In going up and down this country a man comes to me sometimes and says, "Mr John, do you suppose that all the heathen are going to hell?" and his impression is, that if they are not going to hell, he has nothing to do with mission work. But there is another way of putting the question and I sometimes turn round and say, "Sir, do you suppose that they are all going to heaven?" I do not know where they are going, but one thing I am perfectly sure of is that they are not fit to go to heaven; and if I could tell you tonight that all the Chinese were launched into heaven just as they leave this world, I venture to say, my friends, that very few of you would care to go there at all unless you went as missionaries.' In a letter written soon after this speech, John affirmed his belief that God mercifully allows for the painless destruction of the heathen sinner, his Calvinism tempered by time and experience.

The forces of sin and evil which, John felt, were usually kept at bay beyond the gates of the Hankow mission compounds, erupted with alarming proximity during those anti-foreign riots of 1891 along the Yangtze valley. They began in Nanking, spread to Ichang and blew up almost to rebellion size in some places, where missionary premises were burned and looted, missionaries were robbed, stoned and had to flee for their lives. The trouble came like 'thunderbolts from a clear sky' to most people, Griffith John wrote, but he, like Timothy Richard, had long been aware that Chinese xenophobia was on the boil again and that new versions of anti-Christian pamphlets were circulating in the nearby province of Hunan.

Through his many Chinese friends John discovered that most of them originated from a pawnshop in Changsha, the Hunanese capital, and that influential officials were involved in their production. The pamphlets were carefully calculated to stir up mob violence and superstitious hysteria and their pornographic descriptions of missionaries' sexual behaviour were similar to earlier imaginative exercises. Christianity was termed throughout 'the pig-grunt religion', a term originally derived from the unfortunate fact that the Roman Catholic word for God was *Tien-chu* (Lord of Heaven) and that '*chu*' when pronounced in a different tone also meant 'pig'. Thus Christian prayers were pig-squeaks, and garish illustrations depicted Westerners (pig-goat-devils) worshipping a red-snouted hog hanging from a cross and other hogs with erect phalli. They were supplemented with gruesome ditties:

> Fat meat,
> Fresh blood,
> Take seats,
> Feast friends.
> Coarse skin,
> Big bones,
> My teeth grind small.
> Talk of Bishops.
> All make chops.

As a result of John's investigations the Hunanese tracts were temporarily suppressed and the officials chiefly responsible for their production were dismissed. It was an outcome that John could not have accomplished without the help of Gardner, the British Consul in Hankow, who strongly supported his protests to the Chinese government. Such an alliance was fairly unusual, for the consuls were still in the same dilemma of being expected to protect missionaries and quell demonstrations against them on the one hand, and, on the other, to avoid any active political interference in the country's internal affairs. It was a dilemma that reflected the ambiguous attitude of the British who were still the most powerful Western nation in the Far East. Thus they had the largest economic interest vested in the preservation of the Manchu régime and were particularly loath to instigate any form of military operation that might topple it by sparking off revolution.

For the next few years, which included the period of the Sino-Japanese War (1894–5), various kinds of anti-foreign disturbances broke out in several provinces. Missionaries commonly bore the brunt of these attacks – if only because they were most usually on the spot and most conspicuously defenceless – and became an increasing irritant to both the Chinese and foreign secular authorities, as victims, culprits, intruders, relentless troublemakers and incessant grumblers. During these episodes the British maintained their much-used posture of informal compromise – now bristling upon the scene of action with a show of gunboats at the ready, now retreating to diplomatic threats, demands for compensation and the exchange of mutually-unconvincing promises. It was a strategy that enabled them to retain their commercial supremacy in China for a few more years, but it could not be effective in the longer term. This was because other ambitious nations were also determined to enlarge and consolidate their own spheres of economic influence in China and because the Manchu government was, in any case, losing its grip.

CHAPTER FOURTEEN

A Number of Wonderful Edicts

On 30th October 1895 Timothy Richard, who had changed jobs again and was then Secretary of the SDK – the Society for the Diffusion of Christian and General Knowledge among the Chinese – was granted an interview with Prince Kung in Peking. Kung, like Richard, was a tenacious survivor on the Chinese scene. He had been the representative of the Manchu Government to negotiate with Lord Elgin when that reluctant barbarian had marched into the Chinese capital as leader of the Anglo-French Expedition thirty-five years before; he had exchanged barbed pleasantries with several early foreign ambassadors such as Sir Rutherford Alcock; he was again on hand to cope with the troublesome indemnity demands that the French made after the Tientsin Massacre.

Five years after that, Tung Chih, the young Emperor, whose mother the Empress Dowager had virtually ruled the country, had died of smallpox and Kung had been involved in a dangerous quarrel over the question of the Imperial succession. In the absence of a direct heir, Kung had tried to rally sufficient support to have his son proclaimed the new emperor, but he had been out-manoeuvred by the Empress Dowager, one of history's great conspirators, who managed to install her three-year-old nephew Kuang Hsu on the Dragon Throne. The Empress thus continued to rule the country through Kuang Hsu and after a few years had so consolidated her authority that she had been strong enough to dismiss Kung from his position on the Grand Council and banish him for ten years on charges of 'becoming unduly inflated with his pride of place' and displaying 'nepotism and slothful inefficiency'.

Though the charges were audacious in the extreme (it certainly took nerve for the Empress to hand out accusations of nepotism, considering that she ruled China for forty years through two young male relatives, both of whose claims to the throne were shaky), Kung was, by all accounts, a man fully aware of his 'pride of place'. As a young Manchu nobleman he had greeted Lord Elgin with a 'stiff superciliousness' which had at once put that dignitary's back up, and Richard decided that he was 'the most imperious man I ever met, every inch a prince, with a demeanour as if he felt himself a god among men . . . It is said,' he continued, 'that he was the only man in the Empire of whom the Empress Dowager was afraid.'

Certainly she was wary of him still, though she recalled him from comparative obscurity to negotiate following China's defeat at the hands of the Japanese in 1895 – a defeat that at last shattered the complacency of the official classes and prodded them into some self-questioning, if not much in the way of self-strengthening. So, after the war, Kung was back as President of the Tsungli Yamen, the office he had first created, and there, on 30th October, he showed his long-standing dislike of missionaries by having Richard ushered to a draughty seat near the door. Richard had come with a memorial pleading for the greater toleration of Christian evangelism in China and freedom from persecution for converts. Kung listened coldly, said very little and then swept out, which was his disconcerting way; another member of the Tsungli Yamen congratulated Richard for being so frank with the Prince and assured him, 'Your visit here will do good.'

Neither it, nor eight subsequent visits which Richard paid to the Tsungli Yamen on the same errand, were much good insofar as they did nothing to change the course of subsequent calamitous events; but Richard appends an interesting footnote to his account of the meetings which serves as a reminder of how much influence, at least, he was beginning to exert in the country's affairs. Richard writes that the Russian Minister, Count Cassini, had also been granted an interview with Kung about the same time and 'asked Kung if he had read my translation of Mackenzie's *Nineteenth Century*. The Prince replied that he had. "And what do you think of it?" "It is a very useful book to China." "Then I'm afraid you have not grasped the moral of it," replied the Russian Minister. "It teaches democracy *versus* autocracy. If those views become current throughout China, you six million Manchus will be out-voted by the four hundred millions of Chinese and you will have to go."' With surprising equanimity, considering his profession, Richard concludes, 'This prophecy of Count Cassini was realised in 1911.'

Mackenzie's *History of the Nineteenth Century* was an idiosyn-cratic and subjective work in comparison with some of the standard histories of the period, but Richard chose it for translation because it so fervently echoed his own faith that a divinely-inspired alliance between Christianity and modern industrialisation would promote the general good of mankind. 'God,' he wrote in the preface to his translation, 'was breaking down the barriers between all nations by railways, steamers and telegraphs in order that we should all live in peace and happiness as brethren of one family; but the Manchus, by continual obstruction, were deter-mined from the first to prevent this intercourse.'

At that time Chinese translations of secular, scholarly Western works were still scarce; it was estimated that only 567 were translated during the second half of the century, and they were by no means adequate to convey an overall picture of modern intellectual trends in the West. Thus Mackenzie's *History*, which had first been published in 1880 and was already consigned to outdated obscurity at home, seemed quite exciting and progressive to the Chinese literati. Chinese booksellers had usually refused to stock translations produced by missionaries because they classed them all as Christian propaganda and also because they stank – foreign ink smelled much nastier than the indigenous ink-stone variety. But the booksellers apparently put up with the smell of Mackenzie's *History* for it sold like hot cakes – a million copies was a conservative estimate, many of them in pirated editions.

The work became something of a handbook for the liberal

intellectuals in the country who were aiming at drastic social and political reforms. Following its publication, Richard became one of the only three Westerners invited to attend meetings of the newly-formed Reform Club, whose members hoped, in the early days, to effect a peaceful reformation within the existing dynastic framework. Among the Reform Party's sympathisers was Sun Chia-nai, tutor of the Emperor Kuang Hsu, now a dreamy, enigmatic young man in his mid-twenties. When Sun Chia-nai told Richard that the Emperor had spent one hour every day for two months ploughing valiantly through Mackenzie's *History* and was extremely impressed by it, then the missionary really felt he was helping to shape the nation's future. He was, in fact, supremely confident about the rightness of his tactics at this time, but he must have been criticised by some of his colleagues who felt that all this social and political theorising in high places was no part of the missionary calling.

Richard left the capital in 1896 but the Reform Movement continued to gain momentum. 'It was like the thaw of a great glacier or the breaking up of the frozen Amur sweeping gigantic masses of obstructive ice down to the ocean,' Richard felt. It was something of a breakthrough time for missionaries in general and all the societies reported increases in numbers of converts. One reason for the upsurge was undoubtedly that the people, humiliated by their recent defeat at the hands of the Japanese, disillusioned by their ineffectual government, were seeking new political and social directions. But this was a secular interpretation that found little favour among missionaries who preferred to believe that the long-awaited 'harvest-time' was at last upon them.

The leaders of the Reform Party continued to influence Kuang Hsu until, by 1898, he became fully persuaded of the need for extensive change. 'Does not the same man who wears grass-cloth in summer change into fur garments in the cold of winter?' he is supposed to have asked, in one of those typically allusive oriental asides. In June of that year, in defiance of his formidable aunt, Tzu Hsi, the Emperor issued what Richard termed a 'number of wonderful edicts'. The 'eight-legged' essay system was to be superseded, which would mean the abolition of 'parrot-like plagiarisms and shallow theories'; temples were to be converted into schools of western studies; Christianity was to be given official protection; there were plans for setting up other western-style institutions such as a Translation Board and a Patent Office 'for the encouragement of everything that was new and useful'.

In the 'Hundred Days of Reform' that followed, the progressives seemed to be winning and several of their sympathisers were appointed to high-ranking government offices. But the country remained in agitated ferment and the forces of reaction rallied behind the Empress Dowager. On the very day that Timothy Richard had been summoned to meet Kuang Hsu himself with a view to becoming one of his foreign advisers, Tzu Hsi struck back. With the help of the loyalist imperial forces she regained control of the government and the reformers had to flee for their lives. Some were caught and executed; others escaped to exile and lived to fight a later day; the few foreigners who had been actively on their side were immune from reprisals, though Richard prudently concentrated on his SDK work in Shanghai for a while. Kuang Hsu was imprisoned for two years in a cold bare pavilion on the Ocean Terrace of the Winter Palace lake inside the For-bidden City, the winter of his life early upon him because he had failed to achieve the appropriate changes from grass-cloth to fur.

Once the Empress Dowager and her supporters were firmly back in the saddle they annulled the reforming edicts, but did attempt some changes intended to ease civil discontent and international tensions. Among them was the edict published in 1899 in response to strong pressure from the French, which gave official government-rank status to Catholic clergy – bishops were to rank with governors for instance and wear mandarin buttons in their caps. Missionaries would then be empowered to deal directly with the Chinese authorities rather than through their consuls and the idea behind it was to keep missionary disputes out of the international headlines, even though, at local level, it implied greater political involvement for any individual mission-ary concerned. Foreign opinion on the edict was divided: the Catholics welcomed the greater power and prestige it conferred upon them, but the Protestants refused to accept the political responsibility on ideological grounds.

The very idea that foreign bishops of a minority religious sect should expect to be treated with as much pomp and ceremony as the indigenous mandarin seems, in retrospect, the height of effrontery, but it was a period when all the European powers felt entitled to behave in a very high-handed manner towards China. By late 1899 all the country's richest provinces had been divided into 'spheres of influence' attributed to one or other major power who had certain development and trading rights granted to them therein. The proud Chinese were outraged by these intrusions, but their government was so corrupt and bankrupt, their armies so ill-equipped and old-fashioned that they were powerless. And thus it was that the undercurrents of violence and discontent among the over-taxed, humiliated and disillusioned people, which could, perhaps, have been channelled into the constructive reform programmes, found a sinister outlet in the rebellious activities of the Boxers which began during the autumn of 1898.

The Boxers were peasant revolutionaries, members of that secret society of Righteous Harmony Fists who believed that their cult of 'boxing' – more properly, a system of strenuous physical exercises of Taoist origin – had endowed them with certain supernatural powers. They were gangs of ruthless, rowdy braggarts who rampaged about wearing red sashes and turbans and waving red flags. They swindled, gambled, hoodwinked the humble with their self-induced trances, charms, fetishes, mountebank tricks, and there was more than a touch of the dervish about their whirling capers with sword and spear that were supposed to invoke the aid of the native deities. With eyes rolling, limbs flailing, they strutted and stomped, boasting of their invulnerability against attack from Western-style weapons. 'Temple of the iron gods, seat of the iron gods, iron men, iron clothes, iron protection, resisting iron cannon they cannot approach' ran one of their frenzied incantations intended to ensure that any foreign bullet would bounce harmlessly off them. For they were violently opposed to all kinds of foreign presence in the country, an opposition expressed in their refusal to use the very word 'foreign' –

unless it was combined with 'devil'. So foreign guns were devils in their canon, locomotives were iron bulls and railways iron centipedes. Their thinking was mainly on this unsophisticated level, for few of them had had much first-hand contact with the West and they did not really understand the reasons behind China's vulnerability in world affairs.

Originally the Boxers had been civil insurgents dedicated to the overthrow of the Manchus and there is still dispute as to when and to what extent this aim was subdued, to be partly overtaken by their overriding xenophobia. There is debate too about how much of the xenophobia was directed against the foreigners' mercantile encroachment of China and how much was specifically anti-Christian. The verdict is inconclusive; probably, as this widely-circulated Boxer poster suggests, the two elements co-existed: 'Greater calamities still have overtaken the nation. Foreign devils come with their teaching and converts to Christianity become numerous. These churches are without human relations, but being most cunning have attracted all the greedy and covetous as converts and to an unlimited degree have practised oppression until every good official has been corrupted and, covetous of their wealth, has become their servant. So telegraphs have been established, devil-guns have been manufactured and machine shops have been the delight of their evil nature. Iron centipedes, balloons, electric lamps the foreign devils think excellent.' Most of the specifically anti-Christian placards were a re-hash of the scurrilous old yarns about missionaries' propensities for unnatural sexual practices and eating children. The same old superstitions about foreigners' magical powers also cropped up; one of them, that had been current at the time of the Yangchow riot thirty years before, for instance, was that they could cut the figure of a man out of paper and that, in a few hours, it would come to life as a sort of evil genie and go about doing harm.

The Boxers also had more realistic reasons for their belief that the West was not doing China much good. The influx of foreign machine-made materials was ruining rural crafts and industries and putting millions out of work; the proposed extensive development of railways would carry more merchandise out of the country, but, as things were arranged, none of the profits would accrue to the ordinary people; the bolder intrusions of missionaries had resulted in the spread of incomprehensible ideas, scandalous breaches of custom and social conflicts. To make matters worse, the most disaffected northern provinces were stricken with drought, plagues of locusts, floods and consequent famines in 1898–9 that forced thousands to abandon their homes, and the Boxers gained many recruits from those thus uprooted and dispossessed. These cumulative disasters were blamed on the increase of foreign influence which was making the gods angry. 'When the foreigners are wiped out, rain will fall and visitations will disappear' was one of the Boxer posters that appeared in Shantung at this time.

Shantung, which suffered most from these calamities of nature, was the province where the first systematic persecution of converts occurred. A common form of it, as described by Arthur Smith, an American Board missionary, who was living there at the time, was for the Boxers to send ominous yellow cards to Christian homes inviting a meeting with their 'representatives'. This was a polite way of saying that if the converts did not formally recant and pay a ransom, they must prepare for the consequences – the looting and burning of their houses, or being beaten out of the village. If the Christians could not raise ransom money, the contents of their homes were put up for auction and it was pitiful, Smith wrote, to see 'clothing, bedding, domestic utensils (including the only cooking kettle and dishes) . . . thrown out for sale in the street outside the plundered house. The shame, humiliation and helpless indignation of the Christians can be faintly imagined, but it was not prudent for them to express in any way their feelings, and in many cases it was not safe for them even to be within sight . . .'

The situation continued to deteriorate. In December, an LMS man wrote: 'Our compound has today over eighty refugees who have lost all their earthly possessions – including grain, clothing, bedding, animals – and five of our chapels are of no use any longer. Battle fought last week. Seventy killed and a hundred captured of the enemy. Seventy soldiers here now, more expected. It will be a sad Christmas for us all.' The soldiers, reinforcements sent by the government, tried to restore order after such outbreaks, but they were often half-hearted because it was clear that the Governor of Shantung, Yu Hsien, an intense xenophobe, was giving tacit support to the Boxers. Following strong foreign protests, the Empress Dowager was obliged to dismiss Yu Hsien from his post; but two months later she offered him instead the governorship of Shansi. It was to prove a fateful posting. On the last day of 1899 a missionary of the Society for the Propagation of the Gospel, S. M. Brooks, travelling through a lonely snow-bound border district of Shantung, was set upon by Boxers and hacked to pieces. The 'volcano' to which Timothy Richard had referred nine years before was about to crack apart.

CHAPTER FIFTEEN

The Blood of the Martyrs

Chinese and foreign politicians in Peking seem to have spent the first months of 1900 making a series of decisions and revisions that led steadily towards disaster. The Empress Dowager issued a series of edicts that reflected the Manchus' vacillating attitudes towards the Boxers. On the one hand she and some of her advisers, fired with chauvinistic xenophobia, wanted to support openly the rebels' efforts to oust the hated foreigner from the country; on the other hand she guessed – and some of her counsellors were perceptive enough to warn her – that fearful foreign reprisals would result from such a policy. The representatives of the major Western powers were divided among themselves about what action to take and, in spite of repeated warnings from missionaries in the provinces, failed to fully appreciate the seriousness of the situation. They blustered and protested, sent for gunboats and let them go away again, pursued a general line of hoping for the best in the face of mounting evidence of the worst.

By late May the worst befell with a drastic rapidity summed up in this desperate telegraphic plea for help sent by a group of American missionaries in Peking to President McKinley in Washington: 'Boxers destroy chapels, massacre hundreds Christians, threaten exterminate all foreigners . . . Chinese troops useless. Attack Peking, Tientsin daily threatened. Railways destroyed, telegraphs cut. Chinese government paralysed. Imperial edicts double-faced; favour Boxers. Universal peril. Unless situation promptly relieved, 30 Americans convened regard outlook practically hopeless . . .' The senders of the telegram, like the other foreigners marooned in the capital, could at least take comfort in their numbers and the protection of a 350-strong detachment of international guards sent up a few days later from Tientsin; but for the small groups of missionaries isolated in the surrounding provinces of Chihli, Shantung and Shansi the outlook was indeed hopeless – for some, hopeless unto death.

The first group of missionaries to be killed were stationed at Paoting-Fu, only about a hundred miles from Peking. They were mostly American and typical of the second missionary generation that went to China during the 1890s. They were young and inspired by a great sense of moral duty; they had been attracted to their vocation through contact with the leaders of the Revivalist Movement; they were comparatively well trained, mostly from pious, conventional, small-town middle-class backgrounds, they were proud of their status as citizens and representatives of an imperialistic major power. In some respects they shared the pioneering, outward-seeking spirit of their immediate ancestors, but this did not prompt them to 'rough it' in China; rather they sought to impress upon the Chinese by instruction and example, the benefits and blessings of Western industrialisation and culture.

Here Mrs May Simcox, wife of the Reverend Frank Simcox of the American Presbyterian Mission, describes to a friend the outpost of civilisation that her husband had built for her when she first reached Paoting-Fu in 1895. It was an imposing brick residence and inside 'we have got our new carpet down in the dining-room, our organ in the lounge, my writing desk, sewing machine, central table, four rocking chairs, bookcase, two pairs of red woollen curtains on the front and lace ones on the back, also a small table with some pretty silver inkstands on it in the back window. . . In our store-room we have cans of pineapple, gooseberry jam, apricot jams, pears, peaches, cherries, salmon, cold tongue, pickles etc., coffee, condensed milk, butter (120 lb) besides bottles of Melluns Foods, medicines, stove polish, corn starch, soda, tins of baking powder, coconut, bags of meal for porridge, sugar crackers, popcorn. . .'

Sufficient for a siege perhaps, or for special occasions such as the traditional Thanksgiving Dinner of turkey, mince pie and sweet potatoes which the Simcoxes shared that first autumn with their compatriots, the Reverend and Mrs Ewing. 'Mrs Ewing sets a lovely table,' May continued, 'and has beautiful dishes and so much silverware. . . I am almost afraid to invite them here, for I think we can't come up to them in style; but then we are not proud and I guess my cook can get up a pretty good meal . . .'

But though the cook could cook, he needed constant watching if he was not to get away with a handful of porridge meal concealed in his sleeve each night. And the rest of the staff were equally troublesome: 'One day our boy lifted hot ashes in a new sheet-iron water bucket which Frank had carefully painted, and burnt all the paint off. The same day my woman sewed two fronts of two different flannel garments together instead of a back and a front. And later Frank found a coolie, who was supposed to be working for him, lying in the parlour with a fur rug thrown over him. He said he had a chill. I guess he was tired of working. . .'

The years went by. Cooks, catechists, coolies, converts came and went; there were holidays at Pei-tai-ho, 'a place of intense delight where wearied missionaries tarry by the sea in the hot summer months'; there were more Thanksgiving Dinners at Mrs Ewing's lovely table. In the summer of 1898 the Paoting-Tientsin railway opened, which was most convenient for the replenishment of food supplies and household goods. Two years later Boxer bands wrecked all the stations along the line, burned the new workshops intended for the construction of more 'iron bulls', went raging on into Paoting. On the last day of June, the rebels, joined by an excited rabble of city toughs, stormed into the Presbyterian Mission compound, looted the hospital and chapel and then surrounded the Simcox house, where all the Presbyterians had taken refuge. They piled combustibles round its walls and set the whole place alight; Frank Simcox was last seen walking to and fro on the veranda holding the hands of his two little sons as the flames enveloped them.

Next morning, while the poor poked among the ashes for trophies such as cans of apricot jam or silver inkstands, the Boxer leaders re-organised their forces and marched to the south of the city where the American Board Mission was. Three missionaries remained there – Misses Morrill and Gould and Mr Horace T. Pitkin. Pitkin was an exceptionally outstanding missionary of his generation, and his career, to end prematurely that day, was a very exemplar of the energetic, aggressive new-style evangelism that attracted so many. Born in 1869 of a well-established New England family, he went to Yale where he became a leading spirit of the Yale Volunteer Band and attended bible-study groups organised by Dwight Moody at Northfield, Massachusetts. For a year he was the indefatigable secretary of the Student Volunteer Movement; he hurried from YMCA conferences to Foreign Mission Days, from Christian Endeavour Seminars to Open Air Conventions inspiring the young with his 'boyishly direct prayers', his breezy, unfaltering 'consciousness of the Divine Nearness', as his memorial put it. Pitkin, Sherwood Eddy and Henry Luce went to theological college together to prepare for the China mission field and Eddy recalled that he 'would box every afternoon with Pitkin and when we would run our daily mile in the gym or the open air, we would say, "This will carry us another mile in China".'

When he was twenty-four, Pitkin was gladly accepted by the American Board Mission and soon began to clock up his weary miles of Chinese itineration. Like his colleagues, Pitkin had no doubts about the innate superiority of Western civilisation and dwelt much on his feelings of intense pity for the Chinese because of their religious and cultural deprivations. He arranged for a Steinway piano to be carried all the way from Boston to Paoting as a kind of cultural treasure; it was presumably still in his house when the Boxers surrounded it. He fought bravely that last day in defence of the two young women with him, till all his ammunition was exhausted. He and his companions, together with all the remaining Protestant and Catholic missionaries in the city, were executed before nightfall.

A few of Pitkin's Chinese helpers chose to die with him, which was not unusual, for there were numerous instances of native Christians who tried to save the lives of missionaries or other converts at grave, sometimes fatal, risk to their own. Honour rolls and stories of such heroism were published by all the missionary societies afterwards; it does not diminish them to add that such self-sacrificing loyalty to one's chosen brethren was traditional among a people where secret societies had both proliferated and been persecuted for centuries. Naturally, the majority of natives who remained true to the Christian faith had been exposed to its influence for years – like Pastor Meng Chi Hsien of Paoting, for example. He was trained in mission schools and ordained a pastor in 1899, 'a man of strong conviction, of great energy, a natural leader, beloved and trusted by all,' was later said of him. He was away from Paoting when the Boxer troubles began and walked two hundred miles back to be with Pitkin. He continued preaching in his street chapel and helped all the church members who wished to flee. He stayed, but sent his son away with a prayer that he would be spared to continue Christian work. On 27th June the Boxers stormed into his chapel, beheaded him at the altar and exposed his head in a criminals' cage outside.

With this sort of thing going on, large numbers of converts did recant by divesting themselves of Bibles, prayer-calendars, tracts and, in some areas, by buying a Certificate of Protection issued by the magistrate which stated that the holder had 'renounced the religion in obedience to the official'. Others fled towards what they hoped would be the security of Peking, and during April and May hundreds of Christian refugees stumbled into the capital with blistered feet, bundles of clothes and terrible tales of persecution to tell. It was a situation that brought into dramatic convergence the question that the Western diplomats had dithered over for forty years: to what extent were they responsible for the protection of the Christian convert? No flock of chickens could have come home to roost at a more unpropitious time, for every building in foreign hands was already full of missionaries and other visitors who had come seeking shelter in a city that was in imminent danger of attack.

The resident missionaries, as was proper, offered what protection they could to the converts. The Catholics went to the four large cathedrals, in one of which, the Pei-tang, ninety foreigners and several thousand Chinese were to endure a relentless siege for nearly two months. The majority of Protestants were housed in the London Missionary Society compound (including presumably that much-disputed 3-*chien* room) or at the American Board Mission.

Barbed wire fences were erected there, trenches dug, windows barricaded, armed sentinels were posted to guard the non-combatants who stayed inside the main church in a state of overcrowded clutter. The extraordinary scene was described by Arthur Smith, an American Board missionary whose books on China were widely read beyond missionary circles because of their liveliness and a refreshing balance of perspective. He was in the capital during the summer of 1900 and his compendious *China in Convulsion* is the most vivid and well-documented of the many contemporary accounts of that eventful season. Daily services were held at the Mission, Smith says, and the 'speakers were surrounded by mattresses arranged for the night, by cans of French butter, raspberry jelly, bottles of gherkins and numerous baby cradles, while on the floor below stood a row of huge waterjars filled to the brim. . . All this organisation, fortification, preparation, although not so understood at the time,' he adds, 'was a valuable drill for greater perils which were yet to come.'

The perils came in cumulative, logical, and yet somehow quite incredible, progression that must have evoked in the minds of all those threatened the sense of being trapped in an inexplicable and endless nightmare. The main features of the Peking siege are familiar: how the Boxers stormed into the capital during June, looting, burning, massacring as they came; how the Manchu leaders continued to disagree violently among themselves over what they should do about it; how, on 10th June, a mixed-nation expeditionary force under Admiral Seymour left Tientsin to rescue the foreigners in the capital, was repulsed, re-formed and took fifty-five days to get there; how, meanwhile, some three thousand foreign and Chinese people were besieged under intermittent fire from the Imperial Forces and the Boxers within the compounds of the foreign legations. Throughout that period, 'the condition of the capital became like that of Paris under the wildest orgies of the Commune', according to Smith. 'Any one clad in the Boxer habiliments was invested with authority to kill, burn and destroy at will and no one dared oppose. Peking and Pandemonium were for the time synonymous terms.'

It was one of the strangest episodes in modern history, and not the least strange feature of it was the involvement of about two thousand Chinese Christians – aged Bible women, enthusiastic pastors and students, hundreds of docile school-children – undeniable evidence of half a century of missionary endeavour intruded in the most urgent fashion upon the inflammable political and military scene. At first, the converts, being Chinese, were refused access to the legations, but on 13th June the Boxers burned down two of the Catholic cathedrals and murdered hundreds of the defenceless inside. 'All that night the heavens were aglow with the lurid glare of burning buildings,' Smith said. Next day, unofficial relief expeditions organised by men of conscience went to bring all the survivors they could find into the legation area. A few days later, the American Mission came under such heavy fire that the missionaries were told to retreat to their legation. They did so, their converts trailing lamb-like behind them. It was a procession, Smith wrote, 'which even in the terrible uncertainties of the hour appeared to many who took part in it at once pathetic and ludicrous. One could not fail to be reminded of the children of Israel as they departed from Egypt, though so far from being laden with the spoils of the Egyptians, the refugees were, in the matter of baggage, very light indeed.'

Nevertheless, the converts took up valuable space and the overcrowded legation for which that procession was bound already 'resembled nothing so much as the deck of an ocean liner just going out of dock, only that it was on a much larger scale'. It was none other than George Morrison, hardly a supporter of missions in the past, who was instrumental in persuading the diplomats to let the Christians shelter in an abandoned palace, the Su Wang Fu, which stood opposite the British Legation, separated from it by a canal. From then on and throughout 'the siege proper', as Smith termed it, the diplomatic body found themselves reluctantly responsible for the safety and welfare of some two thousand Catholic and Protestant converts in addition to their own nationals.

The siege proper began at precisely 4 pm on 20th June, when the first bullets from the Chinese forces slammed into the walls of the Austrian Legation, and throughout its duration the sporadic Chinese attacks were repelled, or at least staved off, by European, American and Japanese guards and marines, supplemented by civilian volunteers from the legation staffs and a few missionaries. Most of the missionaries were non-combatants, but they helped to care for the sick, the children and the aged, and strengthened morale generally by leading the faithful in services of hymn-singing round the chapel bell-tower at each uncertain twilight.

They also used to the full their well-proven talents for internal administration and were active on the various committees that were set up during the siege's first week. There was a General Committee 'of miscellaneous and comprehensive function', Smith wrote, and committees for the distribution of food, the extinguishing of fires, the deployment of confiscated goods, the registration of able-bodied personnel and the organisation of laundry and sanitation facilities. So many committees of such high-falutin title sound a trifle comic in retrospect, but they undoubtedly helped to bring a sense of order, purpose and community to the besieged. They represented those traces of the norm, at which, when they emerge from a totally abnormal, unpredictable situation, all hopefully clutch.

The most vital organisational work was the fortification and strengthening of the outer walls and buildings, and this was directed by the Reverend F. Gamewell, a stringy American missionary who rode about everywhere on a ramshackle bicycle. His presence, Smith says, was invaluable. 'Early and late, by day and by night, in the heat and in tropical rains he gave undivided attention to the single problem of how to render the legations as nearly impregnable as the serious natural disabilities of the situation allowed.' It was found that sandbags provided good protection against the haphazard Chinese firing and under Gamewell's direction, quantities of them were made by the women. 'All day long work goes on of making bags, bags, bags . . . Little Chinese and foreign children play with jinrikishas and bring sandbags to the front gate after they have been filled, for the bomb-proof building there.' Bolts of Chinese brocades, elegant drawing-room curtains, silken gowns and damask tablecloths were all ripped up in the cause, and the Chinese women 'cut apart many wadded garments whose arms, filled with earth, were used to add to the prophylactic embankments on the walls and house-tops'. The bags were filled from holes in the courtyards and 'one might see people of every nationality hard at the unaccustomed and fatiguing work – a long-robed priest of the Greek church shovelling earth into a bag held by the wife of a Minister, string tied by a little Chinese boy and the bag carried off by the indefatigable and ubiquitous chaplain of the Legation, Mr Norris'.

The unrelieved passing of the days accentuated the difficulties and discomforts of siege life, and the condition of the still-occupied legations deteriorated. The ministerial office of the American Legation was 'in dire confusion', Smith wrote, '. . . covered with dust from the bricks and glass broken by bullets. Legal digests, congressional records, the report of the Blackburn Commission, U.S. Statutes at Large, overturned inkbottles, wastepaper baskets and curtain poles litter the floor, while a bullet which passed through a transom has quite perforated the Declaration of Independence between the 12th and 15th lines where the eccentricities of King George are criticised. . .' Outside it was worse. Flies blackened the noisome area where horses and mules were slaughtered each day for food; animal and human sewage accumulated in the main canal; every courtyard was a litter of shell-cases, fragments of stone and tile, empty winebottles – for a lot of wine had been stored in the legations' cellars when the siege began.

The clearing up of these messes, like much of the donkey-work, devolved mainly upon the able-bodied Chinese converts who were organised into 'volunteer' groups with the word 'sanitation' sewn on their sleeves, whereupon they came under the direction of LMS missionary Dr J. Dudgeon, who must have been one of the most venerable, experienced – and disillusioned – missionaries present. The converts certainly earned the bed and board they had been grudgingly allowed; Smith declared that their behaviour was 'almost uniformly admirable. Instead of being a deadweight to be carried by foreigners as many of the besieged feared. . . they were found to be an indispensable means to the salvation of the rest. . .' They ground flour from the eight thousand bushels of wheat that had been providentially discovered in a grocer's shop along Legation Street; they dug trenches and moved guns; they carried bags and bricks to the barricades, tough horse meat and pony soup to the hospital and the school-children, buckets of water to the laundry that operated in the British Legation's kitchen. Their rewards were meagre: for beds, bundles of dried grass cut from the Su Wang Palace gardens; for food, the hardest of the wheat chopped with straw and the entrails and heads of animals whose appetising parts had been consumed by those higher up the social and racial hierarchy.

All the Chinese were issued with permits allowing them free entry to the legation area from the Su Wang, and these were scrutinised by W. A. P. Martin, former President of the T'ung-wen college. Naturally, he was filled with bitter sadness at the seemingly incredible situation and wrote that when he and his contemporary, Sir Robert Hart, of the Chinese Customs, met at the Legation on the first day of the siege, 'we looked at each other and blushed with shame at the thought of life services so little valued'.

In the second week of the siege, converts were also provided with white armbands with the word 'Christian' on them, to distinguish them from the smaller number of 'heathens' present. It was an ironic touch, as Smith pointed out, for the anti-Christian governor Yu Hsien had been the first to suggest that converts be forced to wear identification labels, in order, presumably, to focus hostility upon them. Certainly the Su Wang Palace where most of the converts were congregated attracted the heaviest fire from the Chinese forces and it has been suggested that their very presence was one of the principal causes of the siege; for by giving them sanctuary, albeit reluctantly, the diplomats had manifestly identified themselves and their countries with the aggressive propagation of Christianity and so herded all the objects of Boxer hatred behind one wall, as it were. Another, among many ironies of the siege, incidentally, was that the defence of the Su Wang Palace was principally maintained by the Japanese guards – the one non-Christian military contingent present.

The Boxer antagonism to Christianity received a further boost on 2nd July when the Empress Dowager issued an edict directed primarily against those who 'have been led away by false doctrines and have relied on the missionaries for support, with the result that they have committed many misdeeds'. It promised that those who repented 'of their former errors' should be allowed to reform, but concluded ominously that those who chose 'to form a class apart invite their own destruction'. After that it was obvious that the converts within the legations, who no longer had a chance of 'repenting their errors' even had they wished, would be massacred without compunction if the legations fell.

The legations did not fall, but neither were they relieved and several of the outer defences had to be abandoned, so that the besieged were increasingly crowded into the small area centred on the British Legation buildings. Time increased the number of casualties in the hospital, which rose to over forty, and of dead who succumbed from wounds, dysentery or malnutrition; time depleted the supply of ammunition, which was supplemented with bullets made from candlesticks and pewter ornaments; time brought the summer rains, and some of the handmade sandbags disintegrated into slush. Contradictory messages and scraps of news, spurious and genuine, were smuggled in from the lost and stormy world outside. Now there were reports of the imminent arrival of a thousands-strong relief force and hopes rose accordingly; they were dashed by the next garbled account of fighting still going on in Tientsin and turned to direst forebodings with the rumours that all China was in a state of wild and uncontrolled rebellion. Then there was a lull in the Chinese attacks; the foreign representatives had tetchy, inconclusive communications with the Tsungli Yamen about the safe deliverance of the diplomats; the belligerents sent in supplies of cucumbers and eggs to cheer up the besieged. It was a very peculiar situation indeed and one that, as Smith suggests, 'put a great strain on the human understanding to digest'.

By early August it was definitely confirmed that an international expedition commanded by Admiral Seymour was nearing the capital, and at long, long last, on 13th August, the besieged heard the blessed sound – 'the deep rumbling of the heavy booming guns of "our troops"'. Soldiers of the 1st Sikh and Bengal Rajput Infantry were the first to come marching, with what style they could muster, through the fetid Water Gate near the canal, and on their arrival at the British Legation there was, Smith claimed, 'such a riot of joy as is seldom seen in Asia and such as was never seen in the capital of the Chinese Empire. Everybody swarmed out to see the glorious spectacle. The Rajputs cheered as they marched till they brought up on the tennis court, beyond which there seemed to be nowhere to go.'

A certain sense of anti-climax descended. The troops had been trying to reach Peking for two months and now there they were on the tennis court with nowhere much to go and surrounded by numbers of the besieged who seemed in surprisingly good nick. 'To us they looked as if they had just come out of some bandbox,' wrote one war correspondent sourly. 'They had speckless linen on, some of the non-fighting men wore starched shirts with extra high glazed collars, fancy flannel suits and vari-coloured ties.' In fact, hardship had been suffered: there were cases of dysentery and some Chinese infants died of malnutrition; blood had been spilled: over 150 foreigners had been wounded and sixty-six killed – it was typical that the numbers of Chinese casualties were not recorded.

When, a day or so after the relief, the missionaries ventured into the city, they found that their premises had borne the brunt of the Boxer depredations. 'It was difficult to find anywhere a whole brick,' Smith wrote. '. . . From all the compounds together not enough splinters of wood could have been gathered to kindle a fire.' The Manchu court, the Imperial Forces and the Boxers had all fled, leaving behind archetypal scenes of war-wracked desolation. 'Huge pools of stagnant water were reeking with putrid corpses of man and beast; lean cats stared wildly at the passer-by from holes broken in the fronts of shops that boasted such signs as Perpetual Abundance, Springs of Plenty, Ten Thousand

Prosperities.' Few citizens remained; those who did quickly put up nice new English signs beside the old: 'Belong Japan' was one, 'We are good people' another, and one temple that had served as a Boxer headquarters was re-named 'God Christianity Men'.

In retrospect the whole affair made the foreigners feel a little sick. 'Almost everywhere was the same monotony of absolute and total destruction, unrelieved and hopeless,' Smith concludes, and it was in this sour and deflated mood that most of the missionaries temporarily left the capital. They were safe, they had not been called upon to make the final great sacrifice for their faith; but in their deliverance, as in the fate of those who elsewhere died, they recognised the working of the Divine Plan. At a Union Thanksgiving Service held in the courtyard of the British Legation on the Sunday after the siege had been raised, Arthur Smith gave the main address. Its title was 'The Hand of God in the Siege of Peking', for, in many aspects, Smith wrote, the siege was 'fully and comprehensively anticipated in Psalm CXXIV, especially the 7th verse which we missionaries sent home as a telegram the day after relief came'. The telegram read: 'Our soul is escaped as a bird out of the snare of the fowlers; the snare is broken and we are escaped.'

CHAPTER SIXTEEN

Miles of Miracle

The Hand of God that seemed, in some places, to withhold the forces of evil during the Chinese summer of 1900, allowed them to smite elsewhere with a violence and savagery that tested the fibre of the faithful to its limits. The majority of those Christians so tested were living in Shansi, to which, in April of that year, Yu Hsien had been posted as Governor. Shansi was an inland province, fertile when the weather was favourable, rich in all kinds of minerals from coal and copper to lapis lazuli and jasper, and so much opium was grown there that an estimated nine out of ten inhabitants used it. They were a traditionally peaceable lot, fonder of money than of fighting, and all the most successful bankers and pawnbrokers were said to come from there. The poor, who hadn't developed the local talent, dwelt in dark cave-houses cut in sloping terraces from soft loose rock. So soft it was that roads, rolled over by centuries of carts, were often depressed fifty feet below the normal land surface into monotonous dust-brown gorges. Shansi winters were long, bright, cold, its summers short and hot; if the seasonal rains failed for more than one year, as they had in 1887-9, its people suffered great distress.

As the inland province closest to Peking, Shansi had always figured prominently in missionary annals, and several mission-aries, like Timothy Richard, had first gone there to distribute famine relief and stayed on. It had been an important centre for CIM work since 1876 and Pastor Hsi's Middle Eden was still there, though the Pastor had died in 1896. By 1900 there were one hundred and fifty-one Protestant missionaries working there, eighty-eight of them CIM members; other societies with more than ten representatives were the Baptist Missionary Society, the American Board Mission, the Sweden-based Christian and Missionary Alliance.

A week or so after Yu Hsien took up his new post, Boxer placards appeared in the streets of several cities heralding the arrival of the rebels themselves, who began to collect recruits and drill them in the ritual pugilistic exercises and the art of whirling round at great speed holding aloft a long sharp sword. Day after day the sinister arcs of light glittered in the sun, for the land was drought-ridden again, the seed was rotting in the ground, parched peasants came shambling into the towns to beg, everyone was restless and tense with the dread of famine. Night after dry night crowds went in procession to the temples to pray for rain and the missionaries inside their frail gates heard the thump of the drums, the measured beat of the gongs, the steady shuffle of feet. Sometimes, as the crowds passed, they roared out the familiar catcalls, 'Foreign devils, foreign devils', and that terrible hiss 'Sha, sha, sha' [kill, kill, kill].

On 25th June one of the many Imperial proclamations was posted up at the telegraph office in Tai Yuan Fu, the provincial capital. It stated that war had been declared against foreigners and the Boxers had destroyed two warships – an act which gave great pleasure to the Emperor. It concluded, 'Foreign religions are reckless and oppressive, disrespectful to the gods and oppressive to the people. The Righteous will burn and kill. Your judgements from heaven are about to come. Turn from the heterodox, revert to the true . . . If you do not repent there will be no opportunity for after-regretting.' This was plain enough licence from the seat of power itself for Yu Hsien and he felt safe to give full rein to his passionate xenophobia. He did it in the grand style by stage-managing in his own courtyard the bloodiest massacre of the largest number of missionaries that occurred during the Rebellion.

All the Protestant missionaries and their families, Catholic priests and nuns and several converts were rounded up and herded into a house in the city outskirts. Their numbers included the

Baptist George Farthing, a colleague of Timothy Richard's, and two mission doctors. On the morning of 9th July they were all handcuffed and marched to the central yamen, where Governor Yu Hsien, surrounded by an armed bodyguard, stood waiting for them. A convert, unwilling witness to the scene, described it thus: 'The first to be led forth was Mr Farthing. His wife clung to him but he gently put her aside and going in front of the soldiers knelt down without saying a word and his head was struck off by one blow of the executioner's axe. He was quickly followed by . . . Doctors Lovitt and Wilson, each of whom was beheaded by one blow of the executioner. Then Yu Hsien grew impatient and told his bodyguard, all of whom carried heavy swords with long handles, to help kill the others . . . When the men were finished the women were taken. Mrs Farthing had hold of the hands of her children who clung to her, but soldiers parted them and with one blow beheaded their mother . . . Mrs Lovitt was wearing her spectacles and holding the hand of her little boy even when she was killed. She spoke to the people saying, "We all came to China to bring you the good news of the salvation of Jesus Christ, we have done you no harm, only good, why do you treat us so?" A soldier took off her spectacles before beheading her which needed two blows.' Forty-five foreigners – thirty-three Protestant, twelve Catholic – were killed in similar fashion that day, together with a number of native Christians; the heads of some were placed in cages on the gates of the city.

The news of the massacre spread swiftly and wildly through the secret, double-edged land, and everywhere missionary families, pastors and loyal converts gathered together unobtrusive bundles of belongings, took to pack donkeys or mule carts and tried to escape. Most of them made for remote rural areas where they lived for days or weeks the nerve-racked, threadbare existences of hunted fugitives, eating berries, drinking rank water, hiding inside threshing barns, caves, abandoned shrines. Many of them were caught and were then hacked to death with knives, stuck with spears or burned. But some were spared or managed to evade discovery, so that there exists a minor canon of harrowing and exciting 'Boxer escape stories'. The unshakeable fortitude of the missionaries, the devoted bravery of many converts shines through their pages to make an impressive testament of the strength of their belief. 'The power of religion depends in the last resort upon the credibility of the banners it puts into the hands of men as they stand before death,' writes a modern philosopher. The Boxer Rebellion was the last historical occasion when so many Christians willingly faced martyrdom for their faith with their brave banners held so confidently high.

Among those who suffered most of all were the Reverend Archibald Glover, his twenty-eight-year old wife Flora, who was seven months pregnant at the time, their children Hedley and Hope, and their companion in extremity, young Miss Jessie Gates. Glover, who survived, described their ordeals in his *Thousand Miles of Miracle in Shansi*, a haunting account of the lingering tortures of dread, pain, privation, panic, false hope, imprisonment, sickness and eventual loss. It encompasses almost the entire range of physical and psychological brutalities which, in some smaller measure, were inflicted upon one or other of all the missionaries who fled, hid, sickened, died during that cruel summer, and can thus stand as worthy record for them all.

The Glovers were CIM members, stationed at Lu-an, a prefectural city south-east of Tai Yuan Fu. From early June Lu-an was restless and touchy, with inflammatory posters sprouting on every public building and Boxers stamping in every square. On the 10th day of the 6th Moon the Glovers decided to flee – which was not a straightforward decision to make. Some of the missionaries who fled were later accused of the cowardly desertion of their posts, but it was not that simple. For there was no doubt that their continued presence in an already-disturbed area tended to inflame local xenophobia and thus further endanger not only their own lives but those of the church members identified with them. So the Glovers went, stealthily packing their mule litters by lantern light, closing themselves inside and jogging unobtrusively out of the city gate at first cold streak of dawn.

Calamity overtook them almost at once, for, when they stopped at an inn to rest, the first of many aggressive, noisy mobs filled the courtyard. Ransom money was demanded and when none was forthcoming, their litters were plundered and they were kept prisoners inside the inn. That evening, headmen from the surrounding villages were summoned to put the Glovers 'on trial' – which must have been quite an event in the lives of local worthies whose concerns usually centred on the organisation of 'crop-watching guards', the repair of river banks or the supervision of fairs and markets. Given the chance to think big, they did so and found the Glovers guilty of just about every crime ever charged against foreigners – poisoning wells, causing drought, blaspheming the gods, using babies as fish-bait, bewitching the ground and other things 'too vile to put on paper'. The unanimous verdict was that the foreign devils were unfit to live, at which a lively discussion ensued about how they should be got rid of – poisoning or shooting were suggested and the fate graphically described by the Chinese as 'that time when the head and the body shall occupy different places'. It was finally decided that the next morning the prisoners should simply be carried outside where the people would fall upon them.

The missionaries waited, sleepless, in prayer; the children fitfully dozed. At three o'clock a gong began a continuous hollow beat; each doomladen thud sank into their entrails. Soon after daylight they were hustled into separate litters which moved forward in procession to the measured gong's sound. 'As we passed out of the courtyard . . . what a sight met our eyes,' Glover wrote. 'The roadway for the first hundred yards was held by Boxer guards armed with sword and spear and brave in Boxer red; while on the other side was massed a dense formation, a countless multitude. . .' As they moved along, half-naked, jeering men clung to the litter poles, their queues lashed round their heads in preparation for action, and armed with cudgels, stones, scythes.

What happened next was so close to a miracle that Glover gave it no other name. The gong stopped its beat and the people hurled themselves upon the litters, overturning them, hacking through the cordage and straw canopies with their knives. Glover and Hedley, together in one litter, were thrown bodily out while the crowd fought for loot; as he picked himself up Glover saw his wife, daughter and Jessie Gates also 'creep out from the midst of that murderous mass unscathed'. He adds, 'It is impossible to convey to the reader's mind any adequate idea of the miraculous nature of that deliverance' – no bone broken by collapsing litter or stampeding mule, no flesh torn by knife or spear. At that point, and with that inexplicable unpredictability which, judging from several other accounts, seemed to be characteristic of Chinese mob behaviour, the people suddenly lost interest in them and harmed them no more. Left alone, the missionaries crawled away like wounded animals into a narrow gully where they knelt together in thanksgiving prayer.

Thanksgiving was premature, for their situation was still forlorn and desperate. 'Stripped of all means of support, seven hundred miles from the nearest place of refuge, without a conveyance or the means of providing one, beset on all sides by hostile crowds – literally we were wandering in the wilderness in a solitary way; we found no city to dwell in. Hungry and thirsty our souls fainted in us. But a few days more and we should be entering the hottest period of the year – the *fu-tien* or dog days; and as I looked at the two weak women and the two tiny children before me, the question forced itself upon me, "Can thy heart endure? Who is sufficient for these things?"' Sufficiencies of faith, of self, tested in the stark times of fire and darkness crumble or dilate; until such times the question is rhetorical. The frail group in the gully on that searingly hot Shansi morning crept forward together into a seven-hundred-mile-long tunnel of nightmare, for which they proved sufficient.

Within a few hours they were again set upon by Boxers. They were stripped of their last possessions and most of their clothes. The children, left with nothing but their socks and gauze vests, ran about wringing their hands and sobbing in bewilderment; Jessie Gates, naked to the waist, lay in the dusty road bleeding from a head-wound; a beggar, who had purloined Glover's gown, offered in exchange his filthy coat for the missionary to cover his nudity; Flora's large white pregnancy was helplessly exposed to the sun and the men's hot eyes. For the rest of that death-dogged day crowds shambled around them, now trailing their tottering steps, now forcing them again to the ground and mounting cat-and-mouse guard over them. The missionaries' spirits remained at a high, nervous pitch; so many of the phrases their hearts had always lived by were written for just such extremities: 'Fear not them who kill the body and after that have no more that they can do'; 'Be not dismayed for I am thy God; I will strengthen thee'; 'Fear none of these things which thou shalt suffer. Be thou faithful unto death and I will give thee the crown of life'.

When, towards nightfall, they were again left to continue their way, one man pressed into Glover's hand a tin of the condensed milk that had earlier been snatched from them; a woman, curious in a doorway, lent Jessie Gates needle and thread to pull together her torn shift. Such impulsive acts of compassion were as unaccountable as the brutal attacks and the missionaries could never guess how any new crowd would respond to their bereft situation.

At the next village they were stoned and then allowed to get away while the headman sent for 'reinforcements' who would, he said, kill them. Seeking concealment, they stumbled away along a stony river bed, Glover carrying his daughter, Jessie helping Flora. 'Two things were against us,' Glover noted, 'the superb brilliance of the moon and the whiteness of the ladies' *san-tzi* (under-garments). Added to this was the almost total absence of adequate cover. . . To this hour I can never look up at the full moon in the glory of its radiance without a shudder going through me. Instinctively and invariably it recalls that night of nights and only that night; and I live again the fear and trembling of our race for life.'

This Glover had to accept as part of the price for his deliverance, that, for the remainder of his life, he must live with the deep grievous wound of memory at the mind's core. The flash of sun on any steel perhaps, or the rip of a white garment, the beat of a gong or the glory of that riding moon and he was thrust back remorselessly again and again to where it all was: back to the dirt and the sweat, the falling and the hurting, glazed hatred of a hundred eyes, wood, rope, stones tearing soft skin, tongue dry and heavy as stone in the parched mouth, stomach crawling with fear and hunger, body sodden with exhaustion, but the mind still shrieking the 'unspeakably precious words'. 'But now in Christ

Jesus ye who once were far off are made near by the blood of Christ.' For what could he, those with him and all the other missionaries who were running, hiding, suffering, dying, not endure as long as that vision remained with them – the thorns, the nails, the spears and the brightest blood that ever was, spilled on the sacred hill?

Late that night, the moon still full, they found concealment in a stony depression atop a high hill, a barren place that the next day's brassy sun burned to a waterless inferno. The child Hope, her tender skin blistered bright red, lapsed into a continuous piteous croon, 'Do give me water, mother. Please, water, father . . .' until her swollen tongue stuck. Flora, most burdened among them, lay in a state of collapse on the searing earth and in the hour that Glover named the bitterest of all the bitter hours, doubted, and he heard from her lips 'the serpent's hiss'. 'Where are his promised mercies and loving-kindness now?' she moaned, as he supported her tossing head. 'Has he not forgotten to be gracious? Oh God has forsaken us.' 'My heart,' Glover confesses, 'was utterly broken before Him.' But, 'scarcely had the words of anguish passed my precious one's lips than God put into Miss Gates' mouth the most wonderful song of praise I ever heard. Kneeling by the side of her prostrate sister and holding her hand, she poured forth passage after passage, promise after promise from the Word, exalting His Name, declaring His faithfulness and proving His unchanging and unchangeable love.' Thus they drank '. . . out of the wells of salvation . . . deep draughts of the pure river of the water of life flowing freely to us now from the throne of God and of the Lamb . . . Our eyes were opened and we knew Him and the Word of His promise was fulfilled to the letter, "A Man shall be as rivers of water in a dry place, as the shadow of a rock in a weary land".'

The strength of that draught enabled them to leave the burning hill and find a stream at which they sucked and sucked till their tongues and lips were plastered yellow with its silt. That afternoon, as they crouched hiding in the shelter of some tombs, they heard the beat of another gong, the shuffle of other threatening feet. It was an official's procession with 'the usual motley crew of the yamen tatterdemalions with their clowns' caps and sign-boards' – one of whom spotted them. They were roughly seized, but were then assured by the official that he had just received orders to find them and escort them safely to the next district. They were bundled into a cart and taken to an inn where they were actually fed with pork dumplings and given water – how infinitely delicious they seemed. Hissing, heaving crowds again gathered in the courtyard outside, again they were told their death was imminent – by burning this time, in the room they were in, once enough fuel had been collected to stoke up a good blaze. But again the magistrate could not quite screw himself up to the murder point and instead, as local authorities will when in a quandary of indecision, he passed the responsibility on by sending them away to the next administrative district.

Seventeen administrative districts lay between the Glovers and the Shansi border, and because they had been issued with criminals' passports, they were totally at the mercy of the power-that-was in each yamen – who could let them pass through, send them back, ill-treat, imprison or kill them according to his whim. It was indeed a 'daily dying' for, as they discovered, the whims of the magistrates were various and terrible. For two days they were borne along for twelve hours at a stretch on flat springless coal trolleys that crashed and plunged down the rubble of every mountain side. Coming to a walled city one sunset, they were left outside the yamen gate for hours, while the people pressed them into the tightest corner of all, tore their clothes and hair, spattered them with gravel and excrement. Sometimes, part of the nightmare, a sinister figure dressed in coarse white calico walked beside them for miles – white signifying mourning, his presence suggesting the approach to some place of execution. On another occasion, pennons of imperial yellow announcing the foreigners' death sentences were attached to their carts and old women wailed a piteous funereal chant for Flora Glover as she jolted by in all her distress. The drought continued and the crowds took up an ominous new chant which Glover rendered as, 'See the rain does not come. The sky is as brass; foreign blood must be spilt. Or the season will pass.'

The sky was brass indeed on the day they first heard those

words, and that night they spent in a filthy oven-hot room, 'its atmosphere reeking with the sickly fumes of opium and tobacco blown from the pipes of the five gaolers whose forms were revealed by the opium lamps, lying stark naked around us'. The missionaries turned, as always, to prayer, and, praying in Chinese so that the men could understand, they 'made a united cry to God' that He might 'send rain enough to satisfy the need of these poor people, and, because of our extremity, to send it now'. Before dawn the rains came and 'the throb of the heavy plash plash of the waters without was the echo in our ears of His own Voice – a music of God's own setting to the new song which He now put in our mouths'. The gaolers were impressed and allowed them to stand in their prison doorway and drink in the promise of that sweet water.

It continued to deluge for two days during which the missionaries were confined within the same fetid room; the third night, their gaolers received orders from the magistrate to poison them with opium before morning. The opium lamps were duly primed, the shutters clamped tight. Glover, moving a fan over the prostrate body of his wife, felt his arm grown indolently mechanical, his head reeled and he sank into a thick nauseous swoon. But the indomitable Jessie Gates, lying in the far corner, did not succumb, and when Flora went into throes of near-asphyxiation it was she who held the woman's head and prayed over her and fanned the poisonous fumes away until dawn came, the sun again, the clatter of animal hooves outside and again the miracle of being still alive.

Alive for the next day's descent of the great stone stairway of the Tai-hang range that divided Shansi from Honan, alive to eventually set foot on the Honan plain and look back shuddering at the ragged rocks of the terrible province they had left, alive with the slipperiest hope of remaining so, if they could just stay the course. The course, for the next ten days, for ten hours a day, was 'the all but unendurable jolt, bang, swing, crash of the cross-country springless cart'. They clung fiercely to its framework, to let go for a second was to risk being thrown out into the dust as the vehicle tilted and lurched. Every nerve and muscle cried out for deliverance, but even when the cart stopped there was none, because Honan was in a state of uproar almost comparable to Shansi, its soldiers almost as brutal, its mobs as wild.

At every dusk they were prodded through the town streets to the yamen. 'What objects we look to be sure,' Glover writes, slipping into the vivid present for a memory still searingly near him. 'I have a nine days growth of hair about my face; I stand in a torn bespattered gown and in socks caked with mud and under my arm I hug the rolled up beggar's rag, purse by day and pillow by night. Miss Gates is shoeless and stockings worn through; the children's gauze combinations are in tatters. They carry in their faces, poor little darlings, the marks of much crying from terror and from pain, to which long wounds from shoulder to elbow bear witness. My dear wife wears only too visibly the look of suffering entailed by her distress – the dysentery which is strong upon her – and all of us bear the deep impression left by exposure, want and sorrow.'

Each forced march ended at the door of a prison cell and a thrust into the black stench of its interior, where the fetters of convicts, caged like beasts behind wooden bars, clanked in the cells adjoining. Each dawn revealed the sickly convict faces peering through at them, pools of urine on the floor, heaps of verminous rush mats; each dawn, they knew, could still be the last. 'So whether it were hamlet, town or city,' Glover wrote, 'we prayed our way in and we prayed it out.' They prayed it through to the last Honanese prison at Sin Yang Cheo, a 'princely place' compared to most, an abandoned temple with a huge gold cobwebbed Buddha ensconced beside tattered drapery and incense bowls. Their gaolers actually gave them some sweetmeats and the magistrate sent over a bottle of lemonade. It felt like a festival when they drank it.

On their fifth day of privacy and quiet they heard the shudderingly familiar sound of carts outside, the rough shouts of the yamen runners. When the gates opened twelve foreigners came tottering in – three men, four women, five children who all 'appeared in their rags, emaciation and utter woebegoneness more like apparitions than beings of flesh and blood'. They too were CIM refugees from Shansi. Buffeted by stone and wood, scourged by sun, their bodies were torn with gangrened blisters, ulcerous sores, flesh wounds, throes of dysentery. For the next nine days they all remained in the temple-prison and, says Glover, 'the ministry of mutual cleansing and lowly "washing of one another's feet" was most graciously exemplified and beautiful to see'.

Eventually on 3rd August, the piteous group were allowed to proceed to Hankow where, four days after her arrival, Flora Glover gave birth to a baby girl; they called her Faith, and it seemed as if the miracle of deliverance was complete. But that was not to be. The baby died after a few days and, five weeks later, Flora also succumbed, the last of the 135 adult missionaries who perished during the Boxer Rebellion. Bishop William Cassels conducted her funeral service in Shanghai, and thus to her, Glover wrote, 'was given the signal honour of being counted worthy of a place among the martyrs of Jesus as the last of the "noble army" of 1900 to pass from the cross to the crown'.

government, their inward-looking society and cultural traditions. The old gods and the old ways which the Boxers had relied upon had again been routed by Western arms and know-how, the power of the Manchus had crumbled and the victorious, contemptuous foreigners could again impose their own terms on the humiliated Celestials. Even the more conservative among them began to wonder if the material and cultural deities which seemed to stand the West in such good stead were not worthy of investigation.

The second factor that promoted the spread of Christianity was the shift of religious opinion within the Protestant Church. It was towards a more liberal interpretation of theological dogma and a greater emphasis on the practical and social humanitarianism of Christian teaching. The doctors and educators were in the ascendant; the itinerant evangelists and hellfire orators in steady retreat. More schools, hospitals and allied institutions were founded and more missionary effort went into such work as the translation of valuable secular literature and the support of campaigns to abolish barbarities such as foot-binding. Missionaries of progressive views came into their own. Timothy Richard, for example, returned once more to Shansi with a new dream of using the indemnity money that the provincial authorities were supposed to pay to foreigners, for the building of a Chinese university of Western studies. Richard lived long enough to see the university completed on a site not far from Yu Hsien's blood-stained courtyard – and that was a fitting twentieth-century climax to the man's life work.

But the complex, diverse twentieth century was not, on the other hand, a comfortable element for a man like Hudson Taylor, whose life had been dedicated to a single, relatively simple belief: that every true Christian should go forth into all the world and hook the souls of the lost from its every corner – not through any feet-of-clay secular agency, but through prayer and the whole-hearted following of divine direction. With that faith still intact, the seventy-three-year-old Taylor returned to China for the last time in 1905. His wife, Jennie, had died the year before and his own strength was slight; it was a final pilgrimage to the land of his obsession. And the land and the circumstance did not fail him, for he died there as he would have wished, in Hunan, the province that had earlier been the breeding-ground for the most virulent anti-Christian propaganda but which was now 'opened' to the bearers of the Christian message. It had been almost exactly forty years since Taylor had paced the beach at Brighton and made the decision that had influenced, for good or ill, the ways of so many. In the eyes of his followers, it had all been for good, his toils noble and fruitful, his life 'The Growth of a Work of God'. Like many another missionary, Hudson Taylor had gone to China with a fierce kind of love in his heart and he, like they, had bravely lived all his days by its light.

A Chinese Chronology

1368   Overthrow of the Yuan Dynasty of the Mongols. The Ming Dynasty founded by Yuan-chang. A time of little interest in foreign expansion. Internal development of arts, sciences, medicine, architecture.

1516   Arrival of the Portuguese, the first European traders, at Canton.

1557   First European trading settlement in China established by Portuguese on the island of Macao.

1575   First Roman Catholic missionaries reached Canton.

1601   Matteo Ricci, famous Jesuit missionary, allowed to set up small mission in Peking.

1644   Peking captured by the Manchus and the Ming Dynasty overthrown. Manchus founded the Ch'ing Dynasty. Accession of first Ch'ing Emperor, Shun-chih. During the reign of three Manchu Emperors, K'ang-hsi (1661–1722), Yung-cheng (1723–35), Ch'ien-lung (1736–96), there was peace and inner stability in China, together with an expansion of trade in tea, silk, porcelain with Europe.

1684   The English East India Company established a trading station at Macao.

1689   The Russians signed the first-ever foreign treaty with the Chinese.

1757   Manchus restricted all foreign trade to Macao and Canton.

1773   Suppression of the Society of Jesus. Consequent decline of strong Jesuit influence in China.

1792   Lord Macartney's unsuccessful diplomatic mission to the Chinese Emperor.

1816   Lord Amherst's unsuccessful mission to the Chinese.

1839–42 The 'Opium Wars' between China and Britain. By the Treaty of Nanking five Chinese ports were opened to foreign trade and Hong Kong was ceded to Britain.

1849–65 The Taiping Rebellion, finally quelled by Manchu Imperial Forces under General Gordon.

1857–60 Two Anglo-French Expeditions against the Chinese. In the resulting Treaties of Tientsin (1858) and Peking (1860) more ports were opened to foreign trade and foreign diplomats were permitted to reside in Peking.

1867 Anson Burlinghame, American Minister in Peking, headed first important Chinese diplomatic delegation to America and West Europe.

1874–85 Long-drawn-out conflict between France and China over the possession of the Chinese tributary state of Amman. China lost Amman in 1885.

1890 China surrendered suzerainty over Nepal and Sikkim in treaty with the British.

1894–5 Sino-Japanese War resulting in Chinese defeat. By the Treaty of Shimonoseki (1896) China lost Korea and ceded Formosa and the Laiotung Peninsula to Japan.

1900 The Boxer Revolt.

Bibliography

Allen, Roland. *The Siege of the Peking Legations*. London 1901
'Anti-Christian Tracts of China', by a Shocked Friend. Shanghai **1892**
'Anti-Foreign Riots in China'. *North China Herald*. Shanghai 1892
Barnes, Irene H. *Behind the Great Wall*. London 1896
Berger, Peter L. *The Social Reality of Religion*. London 1969
Berry, D. M. *The Sister Martyrs of Kuchueng*. Sydney 1896
Bevan, F. L. *Peep of Day*. London 1870
Binns, L. E. *Religion in the Victorian Era*. London 1936
Bird, Isabella. *The Yangtze Valley and Beyond*. London 1899
Bitton, Nelson. *The Story of Griffith John*. London 1912
Bland, J. O. and Backhouse, E. *China under the Empress Dowager*. Boston 1914
Bloodworth, Dennis. *Chinese Looking Glass*. London 1967
Broomhall, B. *A Missionary Band*. London 1886
Broomhall, Marshall. *Jubilee Story of the China Inland Mission*. 1915
Broomhall, Marshall. *Hudson Taylor*. London 1929
Broomhall, Marshall. *Martyred Missionaries of the China Inland Mission*. London 1901
Broomhall, Marshall. *W. W. Cassels*. London 1926
Brown, Ford K. *Fathers of the Victorians*. Cambridge 1961
Bryson, Mary. *James Gilmour*. London 1910
Cary-Ewles, Columba. *China and the Cross*. London 1957
Chadwick, W. Owen. *The Victorian Church* (2 vols). London 1970, 1971
Christie, Dougald. *Ten Years in Manchuria*. London 1898
Clements, Paul, H. *The Boxer Rebellion*. New York 1915
Cockshut, A. O. J. (ed.) *Religious Controversies of the Nineteenth Century*. London 1966
Cohen, Paul A. *China and Christianity*. Harvard 1963
Cummings-Gordon, Constance. *Wanderings in China*. London 1886

Cunningham, Alfred. *A History of the Szechuan Riots.* Shanghai 1895

David, Armand. *Abbé David's Diary.* Harvard 1949

Davidson-Houston, J. V. *Yellow Creek.* London 1962

Davidson, R. J. and Mason, I. *Life in West China.* London 1905

Davies, Hannah, *Among Hills and Valleys in West China.* London 1901

Dawson, Raymond. *The Chinese Chameleon.* London 1967

'Death Blow to Corrupt Doctrines'. Trans. by Tengchow missionaries. Shanghai 1870

Douglas, Robert K. *Society in China.* London 1894

Dukes, Edwin J. *Everyday Life in China.* London 1885

Dyce, C. M. *The Model Settlement.* Shanghai 1906

Eames, J. B. *The English in China.* London 1909

Edkins, Joseph. *The Religious Condition of the Chinese.* London 1859

Edwards, E. H. *Fire and Sword in Shansi.* Edinburgh 1903

Evans, E. *Timothy Richard.* London 1945

Faber, Ernst. *Problems of Practical Christianity in China.* London 1897

Fairbank, John K. and Teng, Ssu-Yu. *China's Response to the West.* Harvard 1954

Findlay, James F. *Dwight L. Moody.* Chicago 1969

Fleming, Peter. *The Siege of Peking.* London 1959

Gibson, J. Campbell. *Missionary Methods in South China.* London 1901

Gilmour, James. *Adventures in Mongolia.* 1892

Gilmour, James. *Among the Mongols.* London 1907

Glover, Archibald, E. *A Thousand Miles of Miracle in Shansi.* London 1904

Guide for Tourists in Peking. Hong Kong 1876

Guinness, Geraldine. *Letters from the Far East.* London 1889

Guinness, Geraldine. *The Story of the China Inland Mission.* London 1893

Guinness, Joy. *Mrs Howard Taylor.* London 1949

Grubb, Norman. *C. T. Studd, Cricketer and Pioneer.* London 1933

Hart, Robert. *These from the Land of Sinim.* London 1901

Headland, Isaac. *Chinese Heroes.* London 1902

Henry, B. C. *Ten Years a Missionary in Canton.* London 1885

Hughes, E. R. *The Invasion of China by the Western World.* London (2nd edn.) 1968

John, Griffith. *A Voice from China.* London 1907

John, Griffith. *Sowing and Reaping.* London 1897

Ketler, Isaac. *The Tragedy of Paoting-Fu.* New York 1902

Knollys, Henry. *English Life in China.* London 1885

Lambert, John C. *The Romance of Missionary Heroism.* London 1907

Latourette, Kenneth S. *History of Christian Missions in China*. London 1929

Legge, James (trans). 'China Famine' pamphlet. London 1878

Little, Archibald. *Through the Yangtze Gorges*. London 1888

Little, Mrs A. *In the Land of the Blue Gown*. London 1902

Lovett, Richard. *James Gilmour of Mongolia*. London 1892

MacGillivray, D. (ed.) *A Century of Protestant Missions in China*. Shanghai 1907

Martin, W. A. P. *A Cycle of Cathay*. London 1896

Martin, W. A. P. *The Siege in Peking*. London 1900

Medhurst, W. H. *The Foreigner in Far Cathay*. London 1872

Michie, Alexander. *Missions in China*. London 1891

Michie, Alexander. *The Englishman in China*. London 1900

Milne, W. C. *Life in China*. London 1861

Miner, Luella. *China's Book of Martyrs*. New York 1903

Moody, Campbell L. *The Minds of the Early Converts*. London 1920

Moody, W. R. *Life of Dwight Moody*. Chicago 1900

Morrison, G. E. *An Australian in China*. London 1895

Moule, A. E. *Personal Recollections of the Taiping Rebellion*. London 1884

Moule, A. E. *The Story of the Chekiang Mission*. London 1878

Moule, A. E. *Half a Century in China*. London 1911

Moule, A. E. *A Memoir by his Sons*. London 1921

Muirhead, William. *China and the Gospel*. London 1870

Needham, Joseph. *Within the Four Seas*. London 1969

Nevius, John L. *Demon Possession*. London 1894

Parker, E. H. *China Past and Present*. London 1903

Pelcovits, N. A. *Old China Hands*. New York 1948

Pelissier, Roger. *The Awakening of China*. London 1963

Pollock, John. *The Cambridge Seven*. London 1955

Pollock, John. *Hudson Taylor and Maria*. London 1962

Richard, Timothy. *Forty-five Years in China*. London 1916

Richard, Timothy. *Conversion by the Million in China*. London 1907

Shao-yang, Lin. *Chinese Appeal to Christendom*. Shanghai 1895

Smith, Arthur. *China in Convulsion*. London 1901

Smith, Arthur. *Village Life in China*. London 1900

Soothill, William E. *A Mission in China*. London 1906

Soothill, William E. *Timothy Richard of China*. London 1924

Speer, R. E. *H. T. Pitkin, a memoir*. New York 1903

Stock, Eugene. *History of the Church Missionary Society* (4 vols). London 1899, 1916

Stott, Grace. *Twenty-Six Years of Mission Work in China.* London 1904

Tan, Chester. *The Boxer Catastrophe.* New York 1955

Taylor, Mrs Howard. *Pastor Hsi.* London 1903

Taylor, Dr and Mrs Howard. *Hudson Taylor and the China Inland Mission.* London 1919

Taylor, Hudson. *China's Spiritual Needs and Claims.* London 1884

Taylor, Hudson. *Days of Blessing in Inland China.* London 1887

Thompson, R. Wardlow. *Griffith John.* London 1906

Turner, A. J. P. *The Cambridge Seven.* London 1902

Varg, Paul A. *Missionaries, Chinese and Diplomats.* Princeton 1958

Wallace, E. Wilson. *The Heart of Szechuan.* Toronto 1903

Wehrle, Edmund S. *Britain, China and the Anti-Missionary Riots, 1891–1900.* Minneapolis 1966

Williams, S. Wells. *The Middle Kingdom.* New York 1883

Other References

  i. Missionary magazines: *China's Millions, The Missionary Gleaner*
 ii. Records of Missionary Conferences held in Shanghai, 1877, 1890
iii. Other periodical publications: *The Rattle,* magazine (Shanghai); *The North China Herald*; *The Shanghai Mercury.*
 iv. Parliamentary Papers 1869–1872, 1900–01
  v. Unpublished letters and journals in the archives of The China Inland Mission, The Church Missionary Society, The London Missionary Society.

Index

References in italic are to illustration numbers

209